RESURRECTIONS

My Will To Survive Is Olympian

Danielle Campo McLeod with Marty Beneteau

Resurrections

My Will To Survive is Olympian

Danielle Campo McLeod with Marty Beneteau

Cover photo by Syx Langemann

Cover concept by Danielle Campo McLeod, Denny McLeod, Marty Beneteau
and Dave Houle

Back cover photo by Jamie Squire/Getty Images

Danielle's first Paralympic Gold Medal, 100 metre freestyle, Sydney, Australia,
Oct. 25, 2000

Foreword

For every hour of her infant daughter's life, Danielle Campo McLeod has spent, by her estimation, 30 minutes in a hospital bed, surgical suite, rehab facility, specialist's office, waiting room or ambulance, often with her life hanging in the balance.

Week after week in survival mode, unable to be Morgan's mom.

The Canadian Paralympic gold medallist and world record holder has run the gamut of miraculous recoveries followed by devastating setbacks; reunions with her husband and kids followed by gut-wrenching goodbyes, bags packed for the emergency room. First-name basis with the nursing staff. A human pin cushion of IVs, blood samples, drains and antibiotics.

Twenty-one days in a hospital bed after complications from a post-delivery bowel surgery. Three surgeries in three weeks. Septic shock. Five days in an induced coma. More surgeries. More setbacks. More tears when the doctors said, "We're so sorry, but we are losing Danielle. You need to say your goodbyes."

While the threat of medical calamity hangs over Danielle, her husband Denny and their household, it has met its match in Danielle's steely determination to survive. She will witness Morgan's first steps. She will teach her kids to swim. She will well up with pride when they take their Roman Catholic sacraments. She will cheerlead when they graduate college. She will watch Denny walk Morgan down the aisle then party like a rock star at the reception.

Because Danielle is too modest, Denny will tell the kids of their mom's glories in the swimming pool, setting Paralympic world records and winning gold medals for Canada. Making her country proud and setting an example for other kids with physical disabilities. She will become the president and CEO of

Danielle Campo McLeod Inc., a powerhouse in personal wellness, and touch countless lives as a coach and motivational speaker, tapping into her all-too-voluminous playbook for overcoming adversity.

The kids will see unconditional love, Denny and Danielle's hearts beating as one; Denny the White Knight, never complaining, joking to ease the tension, soldiering to raise their three kids and two others from a previous marriage while Danielle was confined to a hospital bed. They will find warmth in the embrace of the Campo and McLeod families, for whom Christian faith is their elixir from despair.

But for now, the future is fleeting. There is no peace, only unanswered questions. Danielle needed surgery after Morgan's birth, but following a long hospital stay, something went wrong when she was released. She went into septic shock and nearly died, unleashing upon Danielle, Denny, their families and friends a litany of medical challenges that is both unrelenting and unexplained.

It's enough to make her wonder, why was I placed on this Earth?

To nearly die three times in three weeks, only to be pulled back by medical teams, family and the prayers of strangers?

To feel the numbing guilt of not being there for her kids when needed the most?

To endure debilitating pain since childhood, only to learn she was misdiagnosed, and that the pain could have been avoided?

To question everything?

To teach?

To inspire?

This memoir is Danielle's answers to those questions. It is an account of her many physical, emotional and spiritual resurrections, her sorrows and joys, and how they shaped the woman she is today. It is her path, still incomplete, to wellness.

"One of the hardest things we must do sometimes is to be present to another person's pain without trying to fix it, to simply stand respectfully at the edge of that person's mystery and misery."

Parker Palmer

Contents

Prologue

"Please open your eyes. I need to see your eyes."

He is bedside in the hospital room of his love, squeezing her hand, sobbing quietly, praying for a miracle.

"Please wake up."

"I need you."

"I'm not giving up on you."

Their bond is tungsten steel. They are refugees of the romantic ruins – survivors of failed marriages who met on a beach, courted on the rebound, shared big laughs and bigger dreams, created a blended family of new and not-so-new kids, fought and conquered her lifelong health struggles, only to land in an intensive care unit.

The life-support machine is the beeping, flashing, frightening bridge between the before and after of their life together. Behind its veil, she is in a dreamland of dead relatives and long-lost friends. He is in the here-and-now of heartache and doubt.

She will never be the same.

He will never be the same.

But wherever they go, in this life or the next, they will do it together.

"Please open your eyes."

Where have you been all my life?
June 24, 2020

The lineup at the medical laboratory stretched down the sidewalk into the heat of a Southwestern Ontario summer. I was the fourth of 12 people in line, it was the height of a COVID wave. I had errands to run and I didn't want to lose my spot. But my phone was ringing and the caller was about to rock my world.

A sidewalk is not where I expected to learn that the singular truth which governed my life for 33 years – shackling my body with pain and making me doubt that I would live to raise my children – was in fact not the entire truth. At best, a cousin to the truth. Call it "truthish."

The voice on my phone was my muscular dystrophy specialist, Dr. Mark Tarnopolsky, and he was oddly chatty. "How are you feeling Danielle? How are the kids? It's raining here in Hamilton. How's Windsor?"

Lovely day, doc, thanks for asking.

Being a nice, polite Canadian, I let one person in the lineup pass. Then another. Then four more. I was now at the back of the line and getting anxious. What the doctor wants had better be good, I thought, because I have lost my place in line for the very blood tests that he ordered.

"Are you busy?" he asked.

Yes. Duh. Getting the blood work you wanted.

"Is there a place where you can sit down?"

Gulp. My heart began to race. Mark Tarnopolsky isn't one for small talk. Lanky, balding and probably looking at his pocket protector through horn-rimmed glasses, Mark was the consummate research geek. I knew him for 10 years before he talked about his kids. Now I thought, *What's wrong, what's coming?*

"I just want to talk to you about the results from your genetic testing. Your muscle biopsy has come back and I believe I have identified the type of muscular dystrophy you have."

Really? *You made me lose my place in line to better acquaint me with my illness?* We've been around in circles on this for 10 years. He was giving me so much doctor speak that I thought my head would explode. And it cost me my place in line. I took a seat in my minivan, part apprehensive, part annoyed.

"What I'm telling you Danielle is I found something that I believe means that you don't have muscular dystrophy, but a rare congenital myopathy. And the next news is really exciting."

Exciting?

"There's treatment."

Treatment?

"And you can start that treatment in a week."

Wait. What?

This is not how I pictured being on the receiving end of a miracle. Parked in my minivan at a shopping plaza? No. It would be kneeling in my church, with my priest and a tall glass of holy water. I would be better dressed, and it would be a good hair day. My husband Denny, our kids and our parents would be there. We would group hug, high five and make a beeline to Facebook.

As Cher said in Moonstruck, "This is modern times. There ain't supposed to be miracles!"

But Dr. Tarnopolsky is not one to exaggerate. Research director of the neuromuscular and neurometabolic disease clinic at McMaster University in Hamilton, Ont., he is recognized as an international leader in neuromuscular and neurometabolic disorders. When Dr. T. tells you that your 33-year nightmare is ending, you listen.

He allowed a small chuckle as he shared his new diagnosis – probably a neuroscientist thing. I nearly fell out of the van. The news was entirely unexpected and caused my hands to tremble. How did he expect me to react?

I am a child of the Jerry Lewis Telethon era, and all my parents have known is the fear that MD would render me a Jerry's Kid – confined to a wheelchair and doomed to a short, sorrowful life.

The youngest of three children, I was 16 months old when my parents, Colleen and Steve, noticed I fell for no apparent reason. Kids fall a lot at a year and a half, but it was not only how often I fell, but my odd way of getting up. I had to grab on to something and pull. Compared to my older brothers at this age, I tired easily. My mom thought I was flat-footed, like my dad. She booked an appointment with a specialist so I could be prescribed special shoes.

Money was tight, so while Dad had a fulltime job in an auto plant, Mom worked three days a week for the Roman Catholic Diocese of London. While she was on maternity leave for me, and planning to remain a stay-at-home mom, she offered childcare in our home. She had five kids in her care before and after school, and at lunch, and two for the full day.

Because we had one car, Dad got a ride to work so Mom could drive me to my appointment. She dressed me in a pink blouse and blue jean coveralls embroidered with little pink flowers.

The orthopedic surgeon had me walk down a hallway, stripped to my diaper, then sit on the floor and get up. When I exhibited Gower's Sign – the clinical name for my rising-up method – he proclaimed, "That child has muscular dystrophy."

Mom's recollection is that the news left her in disbelief. The specialist's cold delivery of this crushing news gives her chills to this day. She asked to use the doctor's phone (no cells back them) and called my dad at the General Motors transmission plant. He was still dressed in his coveralls when he arrived five minutes later.

The specialist put up X-rays on a screen. They showed that the ball of my left hip joint was not properly seated in its socket, which caused me to walk with an awkward gait. The muscles responsible for this were already compromised by the degenerative impact of the disease. Unchecked, the joint would wear itself out in a matter of years, making it impossible to walk.

I would wheel my way through life a Jerry's Kid.

The news hit my parents like a locomotive. They imagined the poor young souls who appeared on entertainer Jerry Lewis's annual Labour Day telethon. Mom always set her calendar to watch the Monday conclusion, when the fundraising target was invariable met and Jerry closed with a tearful rendition of You'll Never Walk Alone. She donated regularly. Now her daughter had become part of the cause.

"Those kids die," she thought.

In the parking lot at the specialist's office, she erupted into sobs, repeating three times a refrain from the Lord's Prayer: "Thy will be done. Thy will be done. Thy will be done."

When she had gathered her emotions, and as if to declare war on my illness, and in a gesture that signalled her determination to give me a normal life, Mom took me shopping for pink shoes.

Christmas was four weeks away and Mom worked the phones with the neuromuscular specialist's office in London, Ont., where we were referred for more tests. She wasn't accepting a six-month wait, which would leave us in limbo through the holidays. She pushed until they squeezed us in on Dec. 15.

Doctors were unable to specify which of the 167 varieties of MD I had, despite five days of often agonizing testing. The biopsy which left a scar on my leg, was inconclusive. I was subjected to electromyography, or EMG, where small needles were injected into my muscles to measure electrical activity and the response to nerve stimulation. I howled in pain when those electrodes fired. "Mommy, make them stop! Mommy, no more!" My mother, having convinced the technicians to let her stay in the room, was horrified by my shrieks and appalled by the pain they inflicted on me.

"Why would you do this to a two-year-old?" she asked.

When the procedure was finished, Mom recalls, I took it out on her, turning my gaze away when she tried to engage me. I gave her the silent treatment for two days. Mom slept on a chair in my room, or in my bed, for my entire five-night stay. She took pity on the kids whose parents rarely visited.

Our follow-up appointments introduced us to a world where children appeared in more dire straits then me. At least I could walk. We saw kids in waiting rooms who couldn't turn their heads. Mom wondered: "Is this what the future holds for us?" Fortunately for my parents, I inherited Dad's sense of humour. I made light of everything. I didn't complain.

The internet was in its infancy at the time so parents had fewer means to augment, or challenge, what their doctors told them. Mom turned to Muscular Dystrophy Canada, where a sympathetic nurse urged her to register me so we would be eligible for financial assistance. "For what?" Mom asked. When the nurse rhymed off the array of devices and home modifications that I might require, such as widening our doorways to make them wheelchair accessible, it was as if the volume on Mom's Red Alert was turned up another notch.

Following hip surgery I was placed in a cast that ran from my torso to the ankle of one leg, the knee of the other, for 12 weeks. It came with two openings to relieve myself, but only if standing up. I was supplied with a scooter that would allow me to wheel about on my tummy, but days after we were home I abandoned it. I was determined to walk.

Without a conclusive diagnosis but assuming that I was in the muscular dystrophy spectrum, my parents were left without much of a strategy other than to focus on what remained of me that was healthy. It meant subjecting me to the excruciating pain of physio, where therapists would bend and stretch my ailing

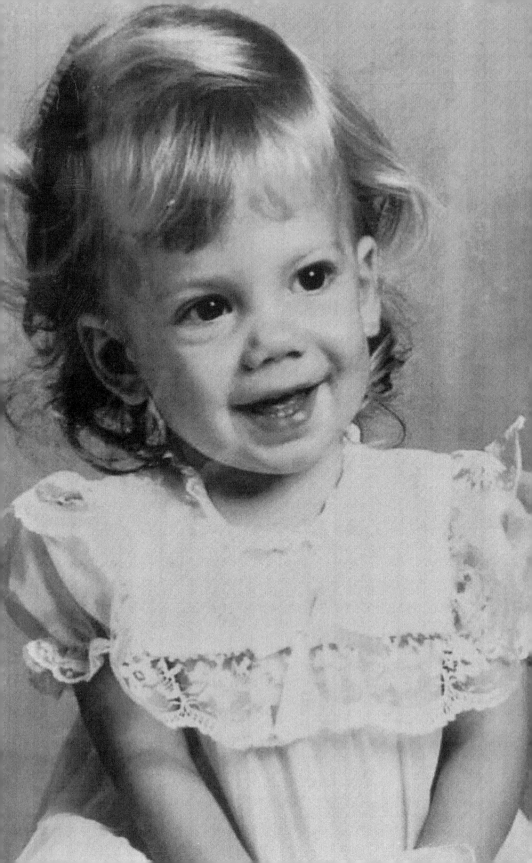

muscles until I screamed for them to stop.

The yellow walls and brown ceilings of the rehab centre led me down a long hallway to a large wooden registration desk and a circular waiting room. Beds with blue mats on top were set low to the ground next to stools where the therapist could spin into position. They carried their equipment in what looked like painter's trays. Straps. Resistance bands. Noodles.

They removed my shoes and socks, pressing the balls of my feet back toward my ankles. My grandfather, Sam Dufour, accompanied us to rehab appointments to give my working parents support. He sat in a chair next to my face. When the pain of Achilles tendon stretching made me cry out, I saw tears stream down Pepe's face too. Pepe had a name for everything, and in the years of physio that followed, we called the well-meaning perpetrators my "physio terrorists."

Thank God for Pepe. He was my saviour, bringing calm to a child's chaos. His upbringing had made him an instinctive healer, knowing the right thing to say and when to say it. Raised on a farm in Paquette Corners, a tiny, flat speck on the landscape outside Windsor, he was the 13th of 15 children in his French-Canadian family. With the weathered face and gnarled hands of a field worker, Pepe had a common man's charisma and a homespun, Depression-era wisdom that belied his formal education. He and my grandmother Tilly laid the foundation for my mother's Roman Catholic faith, though she would say that in adulthood, and perhaps because of me, hers reached a whole new level.

Pepe was frugal, as most Depression kids were. Only with coupons would he buy a McDonald's cheeseburger, his favourite fast food. Nothing was discarded from his assorted scrap collections – not weathered old boards nor the nails that could be retrieved from them. His words were purpose-driven, and to punctuate them, Pepe pointed two fingers your way and pierced you with his stare. He often spoke in the fractured dialect we called Bush French.

Wedded to his beloved Clotilde, or Tilly, he drove a bread truck and retired from a hydro company, where he was a lineman. We had an unspoken mutual respect, as if his eyes were saying, "I know the shit that you have gone through. And I'm here for you." Everyone but me knew – and I would only learn at his funeral – how unique and powerful was our bond. He found inspiration in me and I lived to make him proud.

To distract me on our car trips to the specialists in London, Pepe would have me count the hawks we passed on the highway. He would concoct stories about each hawk. "That one's sitting on a telephone poll, waiting for a little mouse."

With my family at Disney   *With Pepe*

Pepe said a good farmer keeps his furrows straight. As the flat, charmless landscape of Highway 401 sped by, I killed countless hours looking for the picture-perfect lines of sweetcorn and soybeans. Pepe described my setbacks, surgeries and related heartache as "just another load of potatoes," meaning, look Danielle, everyone has their cross to bear. As I shared the front seat of his Buick, he found humour in the oddest scenes, like the 99-cent mashed potatoes advertised on the marquee of a gentleman's club.

"Yep, 99-cent mashed potatoes. That's where I'll be for the next three hours," he said sarcastically.

He loved his cars. He Macgyvered a mirror in the rear of his garage to help him back up. He hung a tennis ball in the front to prevent his wife from crashing into the wall. His wisdom and gentle manner gave me peace in my darkest hours of MD.

Muscular dystrophy packs a one-two punch of pain and weakness. Imagine the aching in your bones the morning after your most gruelling workout – only it never goes away. Imagine the psychological impact of always fearing that you are about to fall. Two steps up a 12-step staircase, am I going to make it to the top?

Your joy is the treasure that MD steals away. All the moments that you think are going to be amazing, or even normal, are subverted by your constant need to navigate. Where is the ramp into that building? How many steps must I climb? Can I wear those shoes without toppling over? Will the braces that hold me upright show through my clothing?

While my classmates gleefully anticipated our daily breaks, I counted down the minutes to recess with dread. They will bolt out the door and I won't be able to keep up. I counted on the kindness of teachers to protect me by devising bogus transgressions for which my "punishment" was no recess.

Because I so deeply craved being normal, I pushed my body beyond its limits and paid a painful price.

A grade schooler is not wired to understand why they can't do what other kids can. *Why does it always have to be so hard?* I often asked my mom. *I just want to do normal things. I'm not asking for a famous life. I just want to be a normal kid.*

Track-and-field day was a highlight of the school year, but for me it was a perverse way of drawing attention to my disability. On my feet for seven hours? Running and jumping? I wanted desperately to compete for those ribbons. I wanted to join my brothers Craig and Kenny as a star athlete. I wanted to be accepted and admired.

Can't I just be free of this weight?

I was not disabled in a manner that was easily recognized, like being confined to a wheelchair. So I was forced to convince the doubters, to advocate for myself even as a young child, because teachers thought, "Oh, she's just being lazy. She doesn't want to write more than a sentence." Well, no, *My hands hurt, but you can't see that.*

The weakness in my legs and hip socket caused a funny gait, swaying back and forth like a duck. It was like honey in the beehive of the school bullies. The more tired I got, the wider the sway. And the more cutting the jokes. My physio terrorists showed up to bend and stretch me in the nurse's office. My exceptionalism was embarrassing. The girls ridiculed me mercilessly. The boys were mostly indifferent.

In the fifth grade, a girl in my class, Lauren, the one who perpetually raised her hand first and shook it like a tambourine, crowing, "Miss, Miss, Miss!" to get the teacher's attention, devised a diabolical new playground game in which I was the principal apparatus. Wouldn't it be fun, she reckoned, to torment the little girl with the duck walk?

"When I give you the signal, everyone run!"

When the recess bell rang, she yelled, "Ditch Danielle!" and it was the cue for everyone to dash off into the playground in hails of laughter. I was alone and humiliated. I went home from school and cried on my mother's shoulder until my blond curls shook and teardrops soaked my pink shoes. My aunt, Karen Demarce, was Pepe's bookend in helping me deal with bullying. Fourteen years my mother's junior, Karen had endured it herself as a child. Because we were only eight years apart she was more like a sister to me. We went to the store together to pick out nail polish. She knew just the right thing to say to make me feel better.

Of the Ditch Danielle tormenting, she would say, "Honey, this is your cross to bear right now."

I had a lot of fear as a child, a fear shared by kids with disabilities. What's the number one thing we tell kids to do if a stranger approaches? Run away. But I could not run. *How am I going to keep myself safe?* We lived close enough that I could walk to school. But when rumours circulated of a pedophile in the neighbourhood and police officers lectured us on Stranger Danger, I became convinced that I was going to be abducted. The other kids agreed I was the most likely target.

It was a paralyzing fear. *What do I do? What happens if a stranger comes?* And once again, as if to put my shortcomings under a spotlight, it was arranged for a special bus to take me to school.

With MD, no one can predict, with certainty, what will happen to your body as you age. Every six months, a specialist identifies the muscles that have stopped working. There was no such thing as good news. It was, "Oh yeah, your legs are still really weak. But now we're noticing that you've developed scoliosis." Or, "We're noticing it's in your vocal cords." My voice became raspy when I tired.

Doctors would convey these gloomy diagnoses to my parents while I was in the room, as if my hearing had also gone. "You know, the heart is a muscle. We're not sure if it's affected. So we just gotta wait and see." I was there. I heard. It scared me.

Learning of children with disabilities who passed away made me doubt my own longevity. I attended one of their funerals and was traumatized. *When am I going to die? Will I have kids? What happens if my body fails but my mind is still there?*

Who will love me?

I tried to live day by day, but that is a storybook concept that held little value for a Jerry's Kid. Boys don't have crushes on shy girls who walk like a duck.

An Easter tradition of giving skipping ropes to the girls in our class led to my designation as the full-time rope turner. I sometimes wondered whether I would have been better in a wheelchair, where I could keep up with the kids on bikes. But I concluded that wheelchairs merely shrink your world.

I fell so much that my mom covered my knees with tennis wristbands. I wanted to be busy, to play with the kids, so I constantly pushed myself to do what they did. And in doing so, I was always answering questions. "Why do you walk like that?"

I lied. *I fell and hurt my ankle.* Even in high school, I never owned it because I was obsessed with being normal. When I did get a bike, I refused training wheels.

Transitioning into new circles was daunting. I was excited to start high school but vexed by the prospect of educating teachers about my condition. Mandatory 12-minute runs in gym class? *How am I going to do that? And what are people going to think when they see me?* Everyone glorifies high school; wearing a uniform will put the girls on an equal footing, they said. At St. Anne High, it was tartan kilts, white blouses, cardigans and blazers. The Grade 9 orientation is where it struck me: *This uniform will not hide what makes me different.* The bleacher seats in the assembly hall didn't have hand rails. I couldn't climb to the top row like the cool kids so I was stuck in the front row with the teachers – where I would remain for four years. Ugh. Uncool.

While grade school was spent in one classroom, high school meant rotating from one to the next. I was exhausted by the walking and routinely late for class when I needed to hunt down the elevator keys. Teachers did not understand. The prom? Try finding dresses that fit over body braces and shoes that don't tip you over. I could not share in the fascination with Rockstar high heels.

I equated the change of seasons not with falling leaves or blooming flowers, but with specialist visits in London. I became something of a medical melting pot. At 15 I was prescribed a back brace for scoliosis, an abnormal curvature of the spine. I wore leg braces below my knees to keep my Achilles tendons strong. The orthodontist prescribed headgear because I wore dental braces. At bedtime, wrist braces completed the Velcro ensemble.

I called my parents into my bedroom one night and said, *Look folks, something's got to give. It takes 45 minutes to put me to bed with all this Velcro.* It became a running joke, punctuated by my protective Italian father saying, "You're gonna be single forever. This is great for me! I don't have to worry about you in all of this stuff." He said it with a smile but I suspect he was crying inside.

No sooner did my parents leave the room than the sound of Velcro tearing away filled the air. I said to myself, *Do what you have to do muscles, I gotta get some sleep.* With its support rails and handlebars, our house in a treelined suburban neighbourhood was not your typical middle-class '80s chic.

My parents' refusal to coddle me was a lesson to anyone raising kids with disabilities. In our home there was nothing but unconditional love – some of it tough – and unwavering support. My brothers Craig and Kenny, six and five years my senior, didn't spare me from a little sister's good-natured persecution. They nicknamed me Smella and happily plowed my face into the snow in tackle football. They did not fight my battles for me, but it was commonly known in the neighbourhood that if you went too far with Danielle, you would answer to Craig and Kenny Campo.

We were an ordinary family dealing with extraordinary challenges. A football was ever-present on our front yard, body contact was condoned if not encouraged, but woe to anyone who damaged the spindly maple tree my mother planted on her 40th birthday, a gift from her dad, my Pepe. It was my safety zone in snow tackle.

We developed oddball traditions born of the mundane. One Thanksgiving, my Uncle Leo whipped up a batch of dinner rolls, hard as beach stones and inedible except for the most desperate squirrels and crows. We turned them into projectiles, staging a bun fight in the front yard. Brothers pelted sisters. Grandkids pelted Pepe. Husbands pelted wives.

My brothers climbed atop the garage for better firing positions. Typically, a youngster took one in the face and ran screaming into the house. Our pet retriever, Boomer, had a field day. The bun fight became an annual rite, often spiced by the echoes of the Campos' fractured Italian cursing or the Dufours' Bush French.

"Tabarnak!"

"Madonna santa!"

It ended when the buns were gone and the ground was littered with overcooked dough bits for the lucky critters.

"We're going to get rats!" Dad complained.

My parents were unflinching in their belief that sports would be my salvation. Ice hockey and ballet were abject failures. Then, at age 6, having abandoned plans for the next Hayley Wickenheiser, they struck out in a new direction. Where can we take Danielle to protect her functioning muscles? Where will her disabilities be unnoticeable? How can we fan that competitiveness that burns in the little girl who refused training wheels?

Where will she find acceptance? Mother of God, is there a place on Earth where they don't play Ditch Danielle?

Sanctuary

I discovered the first of my superpowers in what many would consider a colossal failure. My parents enrolled me in the summer swim program at Lacasse Park, a municipally run recreation centre that was walking distance from our home. Kids in the program were trained to compete. Because it is well-suited to physiotherapy, I had been in the water since early childhood, enrolled in swimming lessons at age two. My parents installed a sports pool in our backyard, selecting the shallower model because neither could swim well enough to rescue me.

The first time I trained with the Tecumseh swim team, the pool was caked with fish flies, a seasonal nuisance in our lakeside community, and the water, having not yet adapted to our humid summers, was so cold it raised goosebumps on my skin. When the lifeguards whistled us into the water, it was if the dozen little bodies were equal. My spindly, disabled legs were obscured under three feet of water. I couldn't fall down. There were no limits. The pool was special, just kids having fun. The lifeguards taught us the front crawl. I found floating easier than walking.

My first competition, at a country club on the banks of the Detroit River, was predictably underwhelming. The other, able-bodied kids were turning for home on their fourth lap of the 25-metre pool when I was still inching along my first. I couldn't understand why the coaches were paying so much attention to me. They tried repeatedly to fish me out of the pool, but I flailed against them, spitting water at them, refusing to leave until my laps were done. As I drew breath in the direction of the spectators, I could see them going from polite pity clap to standing and cheering. *I'm a rock star!* I thought. When I finished and people fell over themselves offering congratulations, I thought, *Why? I didn't win.*

Eleven minutes of disjointed stroking, without much help from my legs, left me completely spent. I had to be lifted out of the pool and carried to a chair. I didn't have the strength to stand. But a wheel was turning in my brain. The pain of exhaustion didn't make me cry. In fact, I liked it. I couldn't define it at the time, but I had found the swimmer's equivalent of runner's high, which is a short-lasting, deeply euphoric state following intense exercise.

As I developed as a swimmer, I came to crave pushing myself to the limit in a form of mind over matter.

I wouldn't be finishing eight minutes behind the other kids for long.

When I began training with the Windsor Bulldogs, a disabled sports club, my coach, Scott Shelestynsky, noticed a second superpower: My tiny, ill-formed frame rode atop the water like a skiff. There was no explanation why. Maybe the scoliosis made me more buoyant? Who knows? My challenge was to find a way to power it. Unlike able-bodied swimmers, I couldn't use my legs for an engine and, in fact, kicking was a waste of energy. My arms, hands and shoulders would power what developed over time into some of the best body positioning in competitive swimming. In the years ahead I would be known as a "pretty swimmer." Pretty swimmers are fast.

By the end of my first season with the Tecumseh swim team, as I continued to finish last by large margins but refused to lose heart, I had shaved two minutes off my 100-metre time. Scott was a lifeguard at the season finale when he noticed me and approached my mother about joining the Bulldogs. Once I started training with Scott, my times plummeted. One day, I clocked a 100-metre of three minutes, 33.36 seconds. It felt effortless. I knew I was faster, but the result made me wonder if Scott's stopwatch was broken. 3:33:36? No way.

Scott knew he was on to something. I was not only naturally gifted, but coachable and not afraid of exertion. If Scott suggested it, I was eager to try. Going to practice, which happened 10 months of the year, was never something I resisted.

I called him Big Bird because Scott, a former competitive swimmer, was over six feet tall with short hair on the sides and a curly blond poof on top. His muscular build was anchored by huge quadriceps which he developed in cycling and powerlifting. A University of Windsor human kinetics student, he was no-nonsense in his approach to coaching athletes with disabilities. In his mind, you didn't have one.

Scott instilled in me that every stroke has a purpose. Fast swimmers find their power zone, the perfect harmony of strokes and breath. They tinker with their hand positions – where they should be coming in and out of the water. Fast swimmers reach beneath their bodies, not beside. He taught me to get my elbows high as I rose out of the water, simulating reaching over a barrel and pulling it behind me. I learned to turn my thumbs down so they operated like paddles. I learned that in swimming, an exaggerated scowl is better at delivering oxygen than a smile.

Sprinters are taught to breathe every three strokes. Scott tinkered with the cadence, so that when I began to tire, I would breathe on my third, seventh and ninth. He used a deafening whistle to keep my stroke on pace: Quick, short bursts when the stroke fell off; long, continuous ones when it was in the zone.

Because I couldn't do dry-land training, I became a lap swimming cyborg. Another swimmer in the club, Tony Alexander, who had cerebral palsy, was training for the 1996 Paralympic Games in Atlanta, Ga., the first to attract worldwide corporate sponsorships and the one which put our sport on the map. The atmosphere around Tony's training was electric. I watched the precision of his routines with fascination, was hooked and started to think, *Someday I'm going to the Paralympics too.*

As months of training and competitions passed, and I worked my way up through provincially sanctioned events, Scott learned of another superpower in his protégé: I didn't get nervous. Big meet or small, heats or finals, I was as steady as a train on rails. While the other swimmers paced the ready room, I made the rounds like a social butterfly. *Hi, I'm Danielle. What's your name?* I realized that in the realm of disabled athletes, I had a trump card: My technique would stand the test of time. I didn't get tired. I didn't get nervous. I never quit. As we tweaked my stroke, I would only get faster.

Because I had high arches, as opposed to the flat footedness everyone thought I inherited from my dad, I was able to maintain balance at the starting blocks better than those who couldn't lean forward. It meant an advantage when the start whistle sounded. We found a way to make my legs contribute to the engine. We worked on endurance. When I joined Tony Alexander in an enhanced training regimen, I swam 100 lengths of the 50-metre pool in two hours 15 minutes without a break. The other member of our super trio, Tyler Emmett, was visually impaired, so his body was not diminished like mine, and while I couldn't keep up with him, I insisted on matching his routine stroke for stroke.

Paralympic athletes compete in classes determined by the level of their disability and rated on a scale of 1-10, with 10 being the least disabled. Determining your classification is essentially a physio test. I was classified a Swimmer Level 7, or S7, meaning I raced against girls who, like me, were generally ambulatory. For reasons that were never explained, I was technically less disabled in the water than on dry land.

S7s put up times that might be comparable to elite, able-bodied swimmers had we been able to take a leaping start off the blocks and execute proper flip turns. Instead, we launched by plopping into our lanes and basically spun around at the turn. Dave Johnson, Team Canada head coach, once said to my mother, "Man, I wish she didn't have a disability because, gawd, she would have been good." She cast him a sideways glance but said nothing, sharing the exchange with me only in later years. There was no point upsetting me with a hurtful comment that was probably delivered with the best intention. Mom knew the distinction between the two.

Mom and Dad split the sport-parenting duties in our household. Dad accompanied the boys to their hockey and baseball games, and Mom stuck with me. She marvelled at my rapid ascension to a regionally, then nationally, recognized competitor. I became accustomed to her voice soaring from the grandstands. Her signature cheer, "Swim hard!", would ring out prior to the race start. Out-of-town meets took place at least once a month, training at least three days a week, 10 months a year. Mom was never home on Mother's Day because of an annual competition in London. I think she regrets not spending more time with her boys.

In spring 1998, at a national meet in Montreal, something happened that would alter the course of my life. I set times in the 100 and 50 freestyle that qualified me for the International Paralympic Committee (IPC) World Championships in Christchurch, New Zealand. If my family had any doubt that swimming was serious business, this ended it.

While my mom signed documents authorizing my joining Team Canada – which essentially signed away parenting rights to the coaches – Dad came to grips with our new reality. It wasn't supposed to happen this fast. I shaved seconds off my personal best to qualify. Seconds don't melt off an elite swimmer overnight.

Dad, I made the World team! And it's in New Zealand! In October!

"Oh good honey. Say that again. Where?

Christchurch, New Zealand.

Paralympic athletes are not allowed family chaperones, but a 13-year-old making the team was uncharted waters for Swimming Canada. And our backyard pool would vaporize before my mother allowed her teenager to go hemisphere jumping without her. She applied for an exemption, which was granted. Between travel, training and competition, Mom and I would spend a month together on an island in the southwest Pacific, a 20-hour flight from home, land of the indigenous Maori culture, the vaunted All Blacks rugby team (and their famous Haka war dance), ubiquitous sheep farms that are the subject of much ribbing, Manuka honey and kiwifruit. Which is to say, Mom would have a great time sightseeing while I would grind out laps in the practice pool.

Christchurch was only weeks away. Now training at a club of able-bodied swimmers, no longer the fastest kid in the pool, I stood out for the wrong reasons. Surrounded by 50 sharks competing for lap space, 13-year-old hormones kicking in, I struggled. I was at first coddled, exempted from the pool chores other kids did, which created animosity. Then at a time trials event, I was slotted to swim with able-bodied eight-year-olds, who were deemed roughly at my level. In a crowded pool, the organizers said, it's important to keep the trains running on time.

I didn't see it that way. I was embarrassed and would have preferred to lose badly to kids my age. At times like these, I learned a lot from my parents about dealing with adversity. Dad's family emigrated from Italy when he was eight and he considered himself fortunate to land the GM transmission job. He was competitive but pragmatic, a make-lemonade-from-lemons kind of guy. He was both what my family called a rage-a-saurus – prone to loud outbursts if a chair was out of place – and an unrepentant crier.

Mom had suffered hardships and I considered her unbreakable. Her mother died suddenly, at age 46, of complications from arthritis, when Mom was 22. Her sister suffered from mental health issues. And then along came me, from flat-footed blond cutie to a disabled Jerry's Kid in the span of one doctor examination. I often thought, *That woman has every reason to curl up in a corner.* Instead, as a bereavement counsellor with the Canadian Mental Health Association, she aided families who had lost children. She leaned heavily on her Roman Catholic faith, and as my swimming career was becoming international, would tell me, "You can go anywhere in the world, Danielle, and the mass is still the same."

Mom was also stealthy. She would address issues such as accessibility without me knowing, focusing on the self-esteem without making the task itself easier. She asked teachers to give me extra textbooks so I had a set at home and wouldn't have to carry them to and from school, but she didn't do my homework for me. In adulthood, Mom might carry my laundry basket down the stairs but stop short of putting the clothes in the machine.

If she cried when I was bullied – and I know she did – it was never in front of me.

At the time trial, as I whined about swimming with kids five years younger, chewing on their goggle straps, mom worked behind the scenes, suggesting to a volunteer, "C'mon, let's use some common sense. We're not going to make her race against eight-year-olds." The organizers didn't see it that way. I was swimming against the clock, they said, not the kids next door.

Sitting face-to-face at the dinner table and still blubbering, I was given a reality check by my dad. Guess what, honey, life is tough and people can be cruel, sometimes intentionally, sometimes not. Deal with it. Own it.

But they should know, Dad, that I need to swim with kids my age.

He wasn't buying it. Why waste energy on a battle for your lane assignment when the real challenge is to lower your time? he argued.

"You want to wear that Maple Leaf, you earn it. You earn how people are going to see you. You can sit in a corner and cry, or you can focus on the job ahead. Focus on the clock – it doesn't matter who's in the lanes around you. There's always going to be injustice. You have to change how you react to it."

Dad got a dose of his own medicine when he threatened to restrict my swimming if my grades didn't improve. My mother had chosen her battle, pushing in all her chips on my swimming. It was what I lived for and I was good at it, she argued. The books would take care of themselves.

Dad could only shrug. "It's a losing battle. You two have already joined forces."

But his wisdom wasn't wasted. I decided that the swim club coddling was over. No more special treatment on pool chores. No breaks on the training regimen. As my dad often said, drawing from his bag of truisms, you don't win silver, you lose gold. If the swimming establishment wanted to devote more resources to my development, I would take it without guilt or apprehension.

Because I qualified for the world championships, I received special attention from the club's new coach, Mike Moore, who had recently arrived from Toronto. He was intrigued by my results in Montreal.

In appearance and manner, Mike was the anti-Scott, soft spoken with a shorter, finer build and curly, strawberry blond hair that cascaded down to his waistline, usually worn in a ponytail. At first blush, I wondered if this hippie dude knew anything about competitive swimming. He didn't look the part.

To my surprise, our coach-competitor chemistry clicked instantly. Building on Scott's stroke architecture, Mike developed drills that leveraged my strengths in sprint racing. While the able-bodied swimmers were given eight-length segments, mine would be modified with brief rests at each wall to accentuate the final kick that is vital to a sprinter. He trained me to use my legs to maintain balance, having me kick twice with the left, which was stronger, for every one of the right. A drifting leg could throw me off course, he said. To illustrate what he called "snaking leg," Mike threaded a pool noodle down the back of my swimsuit. If it fell out, I was snaking. He labelled the three-ring binder that contained my ever-evolving training routine "Campo Mania."

While Scott was a master of the technical, Mike taught me something more difficult for most swimmers to grasp – a feel for the water. Many of his drills were performed with my eyes closed. I would listen, eyes shut, to the sound of an able-bodied swimmer, Ryan Donally, so I could mimic his rhythm. We became training partners and I would draft in Ryan's wake if I needed a rest. Tall and muscular with curly brown hair and baby-faced good looks, Ryan was a stud athlete who opted for professional hockey over a surefire track to Olympic swimming. That he was my training partner and best swimming friend must have irritated the other girls, who worshipped him.

For all intents and purposes, Ryan was my third brother and I cared for him like one. We talked on the phone for hours – too long in the opinion of Coach Mike, who didn't appreciate my late nights. We could go weeks without seeing each other, then slip back into our rhythm. We respected each other's athleticism. We were unafraid to call each other out.

As sweet as he was off the ice, on it, as captain of the Ontario Hockey League's Windsor Spitfires, my mild-mannered mate turned into a crazy-eyed, fist-flying enforcer.

He showed up on the morning of my last practice before leaving for Christchurch, which was optional for everyone but me, declaring, "You should never have to swim alone."

My family all but adopted Coach Mike, who was enamoured with my mother's pasta sauce. He visited us at our cottage in Bayfield, on Lake Huron, in the summer. So I could train in a 50-metre pool, he drove me to Oakland University in suburban Detroit every Saturday in his silver Camaro, Wheat Kings from the Canadian rock band Tragically Hip blasting from his stereo.

At the dinner table one night, my brother Kenny asked about getting a tattoo, to which my dad replied that only if you make the National Hockey League, or the Olympics, will you be allowed. My brothers were average hockey players and I was heading to a world championship, so guess who had the inside track? The arrival of a large cardboard box on our front porch was my validation. It was my kit from Swimming Canada, containing everything I would need for Christchurch. Never had a courier's delivery created such a stir.

The family gathered around as I spread its contents on the living room floor: Red and white track suits complete with socks, T-shirts and footwear; jackets and hoodies; bathing suits, towels and an array of goggles. Coolest of all were the 50 swim caps with my last name printed below the Maple Leaf in bold block letters.

CAMPO.

Accompanying the gear were instructions on which outfit to wear for each occasion, what to pack in carry-on and checked bags, how to dress for the flight. Pepe wept as I modelled the outfits and coach Mike, mindful of his unrealized ambitions as a competitive swimmer, reminded me of their significance.

"Never forget, you earned these. Very few people can say that."

At the airport, Dad and I shared a long, tearful embrace, which, for some reason, I found odd until I realized what he was saying goodbye to. His only daughter was stepping out of the shadow of her painful, awkward and challenging life and on to a stage that would transform her. Regardless of my results, I would be an international athlete with the Maple Leaf above her heart. I would discover an enchanting world far removed from Tecumseh, Ont. I would forge lifetime friendships. No physio regimen could match the healing tonic that was coming to my soul.

"Have fun, do your work," Dad said, not one to go off script. "Remember, we have a need for speed."

Right Dad. Got it.

The Spark Plug of Canada

New Zealand's Maori name, Aotearoa, means the land of the long white cloud. To a 13-year-old on her first trip abroad, the lush green countryside was mesmerizing. No wonder they used it as the setting for Middle-earth in Lord of the Rings. On a surprise sightseeing tour before the world championships began, we were introduced to a Maori tribe and attended a maere, or sacred place that serves religious purposes in Polynesian societies. We sat in a circle, watching spear-carrying men perform aboriginal songs and dances.

While I was too young to grasp its importance, in later years, when I worked as a counsellor with the Children's Aid Society, I made the connection between aboriginal spirituality and family healing.

On our return trip to the athletes' village, we pulled over to take photos of a sheep farm where the barn was adorned with Canadian and New Zealand flags. Sheep are everywhere on the island, once estimated to number in excess of 30 million – about six per human. I reached out to steady myself on a fence, only to learn that it was more than wire keeping those fur balls inside. The jolt of electricity hurt like hell.

At the opening ceremonies for 678 competitors from 51 countries, which wound through the Christchurch town square, while teammates whipped Frisbees into the audience in a Canadian tradition, I balanced a pile of them on my head. I was young and precocious, having a blast with people who shared the bond of disability with me, and who were elite in their sport. I was discovering that I love the stage. And I love people. The next day, the front page of the local newspaper carried a photo of the Canadian cutie sporting Frisbees on her head, with the caption, "The Spark Plug of Canada." A thread that, technically, began on the sheep farm now became my brand and identity throughout the Games, and I would earn it. I signed my first autograph on one of those plastic discs.

If the opening ceremonies were my coming-out party, the swimming venue at Queen Elizabeth Park was my centre stage. I had never swum under television lights, so the pool was blindingly illuminated, giving its black floor tiles the look of a coral reef and the colder-than-accustomed water a dark hue. The pool looked endlessly deep. Everything about the venue, from its scoreboards to the broadcast booth, screamed "big time."

On the starting blocks in Lane 4 of the 50-metre freestyle final, I stared up at the towering profile of Kristin Hakonardottir. One of Iceland's most decorated Paralympians, the defending champion and a veteran who had been racing at the international level for 10 years, Hakonardottir was straight out of Vikings central casting, a scowling, auburn-haired shield maiden in black polyester. Her resting bitchface, which was awesome, was matched by robotic mannerisms, saluting the audience as she would a military platoon.

She cast a dismissive glance my way. "Look at you. You are so little," she said. "What are you going to do?

She was right. I was a waif, weighing 80 pounds with an ill-fitting swimsuit and amateurish goggles that I had refused to exchange for a more modern Speedo design. I looked like a refugee from a Saturday morning tadpole class. I had no international experience, no pedigree, and had only recently broken 40 seconds in the 50 freestyle. On the surface I was no one to fear, other than posting a strong time in my morning heat. I was supposed to be in Christchurch to gain experience, with success to come down the road. So modest were my expectations that I didn't bother to bring my Team Canada podium jacket to the pool. While everyone else in the ready room was psyching up under headphones and transfixed expressions, visualizing each stroke, I was making the rounds introducing myself to anyone who would listen – competitors, officials, the janitor.

It was the evening of Oct. 18, 1998. For the first time in my career, I was racing against a full field of S7 athletes. Unlike other events when swimmers of varying levels shared the pool, and the winner was determined by a handicapping system, at the Worlds it was first to the finish. The 50 is known as splash and dash for good reason. The silence that followed the ready signal was broken by a solitary voice, my mother's, waving her "Danielle Campo, Tecumseh, Ontario" sign and shouting, "Swim hard!"

The time it takes to cover one length of an Olympic pool does not afford much introspection, but when I hit that cold water, magical things happened.

Whereas most Paralympic meets are equal parts competition and public awareness campaign, this one was all about, in my dad's words, the need for speed, where finishing second only means you didn't finish first. I was exhilarated by the purity of mission. Just win.

In Canada, my introductions always ended with "...who suffers from muscular dystrophy." At the world championships, it ended with the country whose flag was on my chest. And because I was 13 and having the time of my life, it was easy to be good. Everything else in my life had been a series of shitty events and how I overcame them. Swimming was, dive in, do what you trained for, win the gold. Woot woot! You're the best on the planet!

From the second I broke the water, my stroke was in rhythm. My mind slowed down. The power zone that we had worked so hard to develop, kicked in. For the first time, I experienced what swimmers call the power rhythm bounce, which means your legs, torso and arms are in perfect harmony as you skip across the water like a stone.

I had no nerves, only desire. *I love this. I want this.* The feeling of sheer power is one I struggle to describe, but imagine a Jerry's Kid rising up from her wheelchair, eating Popeye's spinach and smashing down a door. Hakonardottir was in my rearview from the get-go. I started to pull away, rolling those imaginary barrels beneath me at a breakneck pace. The crowd came to life in a deafening roar, as if they knew that not only was the elfin Canadian going to win, but she was going to make history.

30 metres... 20 metres ... 10 metres ... touch. Look left. Look right. Listen.

"Danielle Campo, Canada. Time: 34.95 seconds. World record."

Jesus Christ, I won. I really won?

I slapped the water, punched the sky and let out a howl that would make the Maori proud. And in that instant, all the hurt of my childhood, of feeling like I don't belong, of literally struggling to find my lane, was swept aside in an emotional tsunami. The little handicapped kid from Canada was a world champion. The best.

And with the euphoria came one more strange, impossible-to-describe but very cool sensation: *So, this is what popular feels like.* I had what every competitive swimmer covets: Respect. Pool respect. I would never again be underestimated.

Among the competitors who gathered to congratulate me was Kakonardottir, the Ice Queen. She shook my hand and said, "Holy crap. You may be little, but little is fast!" I forced a smile when in reality, I couldn't wait to kick her ass again in the next event.

Watching the Canadian flag raised to the rafters and our anthem played, I didn't grasp the gravity of what I had accomplished; only that I wanted that feeling again. I craved the podium. Dad was excited when I reached him on the phone but reminded me there were swims still to come. As always, he was my competitive compass.

A rival coach said he couldn't wait to see what else I accomplished in Christchurch, and I didn't disappoint. I won gold in the 100-metre freestyle, beating the Ice Queen again, and anchored the gold-medal-winning 4X100 metre freestyle and medley relays, establishing three more world records.

Grasping that her daughter's life had entered a new chapter, my mother tried to create a Hallmark moment on the flight home. "How are you feeling? What does this moment mean to you? Some people will never go to New Zealand, so how will you remember it most?" Although the significance of Christchurch would resonate with me years later, my 13-year-old self wasn't equipped to process Danielle 2.0.

I replied, *I saw a lot of sheep and got electrocuted by a fence*

A crowd of friends and family, wearing foam "World Champ" medals and chanting my name, greeted me at the airport and I was chauffeured home in a fire engine, lights flashing and sirens blaring. Pepe arranged for a large welcome sign on our front lawn, which he promptly moved to his front lawn after my arrival. We ate pizza and strawberry cake. Since I had missed Halloween, my cousins gave me the candy they collected on my behalf.

My schoolmates greeted me with a chorus of, I Believe I Can Fly, as I arrived, in my Team Canada podium suit and with four medals around my neck, for a surprise assembly. My friends huddled close to me so they could make the TV news. I argued with my mom about wearing my medals, that Olympic athletes typically carry them in their hand rather than draped around their necks. In reality I found the celebration embarrassing, only worsened by the medals clanging and my pant legs swooshing due to my awkward walk. For a 13-year-old, already self-conscious about her gait, parading past a gauntlet of grade schoolers was mortifying – medals or no.

School children have short memories. In my speech I mentioned being zapped by a fence, which made me cool – for about one hour. Then I returned to the awkward kid with the funny walk. I am the fastest S7 Paralympic freestyler on the planet, which is awesome, except that it changes the perception of me outside the pool, where I'm still suffering from muscular dystrophy. It was hard for others to accept that a world-class athlete has a care in the world.

In a sense, Christchurch made my disability more invisible.

It also placed me firmly in the generous, protective and image-conscious bosom of Swimming Canada. As a "carded" athlete, accepted into the Sport Canada Athlete Assistance Program, I was entitled to $1,100 a month for enhanced training. My job was to swim fast and Swimming Canada would take care of the rest. Thirsty? We'll fetch you water. Tired? We'll arrange a nap. When those medals were hung around my neck, I bid adieu to the real world of day jobs and self-sufficiency and would not return to it for eight years.

After a one-week break, I was back into hardcore training for the 2000 Paralympics in Sydney, Australia, with Coach Mike and a training regimen supplied by Swimming Canada. We did 10-day training camps at Brock University in St. Catharines, augmented by trips to Arizona and Florida and an array of intra-squad competitions. My eyes were opened to the gamesmanship of international competition, where a swimmer might be instructed to deliberately lose an event, or skip the event in which they are favoured, to throw off the snooping competition from other powerhouses such as Australia.

At the Olympic trials in Montreal, the talk of the event was Speedo debuting its Fastskin swimsuit, designed to provide the water-repellent effect of sharkskin, at $500 a pop. The suits were good for a single race and then would lose their skintight fit and be discarded. Having not yet qualified for Team Canada, I was on the hook for my swim gear and begged my mother to buy one.

"Five hundred dollars for a bathing suit that you wear once, and then it's garbage? Are you kidding me?" she said.

When I replied, *If I don't make the team we will always wonder...,* out came the credit card. And not just the cheaper, legless version. The swimmer who didn't use her legs talked her mom into the knee-length suit, because that's what the cool kids were wearing.

"Just please don't tell your dad."

I finished second in my 50-metre qualifying heat wearing a traditional suit, donned the Fastskin for the final, winning in world record time, then – horror – recycled it for the 400 freestyle, smashing the world record by 30 seconds. As my mom said, "It's like milk. It doesn't expire on the day they say." I left Montreal qualified to represent Canada in the 50, 100, 400 and relays, and with a $500 swimsuit that was bound for the rag box.

Reunited in Windsor with Coach Mike, we resumed our quest for faster times. One day, he noticed a quirk in my posture: I favoured my left leg, which was rated at 52 per cent of an able-bodied person but was more than twice as strong as my right. We devised a new start position modelled after a track sprinter, in which I placed my left foot slightly behind my right so I could push off with it. My right foot was so weak that I needed both hands to place it on the block. We made a similar tweak to my flip turn, pushing off with my left foot as I rolled into my power stroke.

Mastering these techniques was painstaking. Once, in a training session, I went off course after the turn and crashed so hard into the lane guide that my goggles became lodged in the rope. But by training us like able-bodied athletes, while the rest of the world was still treating its Paralympians with kid gloves, Canada would dominate the Games. Our team was stacked with world champions and world-record holders.

The Paralympics are staged immediately after the Olympic Games. While the Olympics were playing out in Sydney, our team tuned up at a two-week training camp in Cairns. The gateway to Australia's Great Barrier Reef in North Queensland put the sheep-farm trip in New Zealand to shame. On a break from training we took a boat tour to the reef and snorkelled its warm waters.

I was struck by the blackness of the abyss and the warning from our guides not to wander too deep to be rescued. Imagine yourself in the most perfectly manicured tropical fish tank and you'll know what swimming the Great Barrier Reef feels like.

I forced myself to push past my fear of open-water swimming and the menacing looking fish that accompany it. *You can't not swim in the Great Barrier Reef.*

The jaw-dropping scenery of this tropical paradise, with its waterfalls, rainforest and reef-lined islands, cast a spell on me. I told my parents that I wasn't leaving Australia. I hit it off with the family that owned the seaside Best Western where we stayed, who were impressed at the grace with which I handled my disability and anointed me their honorary daughter. At least I had a place to stay if I made Oz my permanent home.

The celebrity treatment our team received fuelled my budding independence. I told my folks *I was meant to live here.* Mom made the coaches swear that I would be aboard that plane when Team Canada departed.

It was at training camp that the coaches who hadn't seen me since Christchurch noticed a shocking change.

I had morphed from dorky child – I would rate my 13-year-old self the equivalent of a homely boy – into a taller, blonder, shapelier teenage hottie. I carried myself differently. I had my nails done and tended dutifully to my long golden locks. My dental braces were off and I ditched my horn-rimmed glasses for contact lenses. While in my early days of swimming I attended practice wearing Winnie the Pooh one-piece pajamas, now it was fashionable track suits and Oakley shades.

My transformation from Christchurch, left, to Sydney turned heads on Team Canada

"What are they putting in the water in Windsor?" a male team official said, reflecting what at the time was considered jocular humour but would in today's social norms be frowned upon.

What made me even more appealing was that I was oblivious to my looks. Like pool speed, being attractive came easy. I didn't exploit it. I didn't weaponize it.

The blossoming of womanhood struck fear into the coaches: Those Aussie lotharios are going to have a field day with the gregarious Danielle, they thought. The team surrounded me with an invisible wall of restrictions. Unlike the other athletes, I was barred from leaving the team block.

Their reasoning made no sense to me, as I still considered myself one of the guys. It was left to my old friend and training mate, Benoit Huot, of St. Lambert, Que., to point out that I no longer resembled the prototypical disabled athlete. When I asked him why my practice lane was always so crowded, he said in a thick French-Canadian accent, "If you don't like it, stop looking like a supermodel."

With my friend and teammate Benoit Huot

34

Swimming Canada's marketing department surely noticed. In the months ahead, I would become their golden girl in more than a medal sense – fast *and* pretty, the preferred choice for photo shoots, sponsor meet-and-greets and audience development. "You're a disabled athlete in able-bodied clothing," they would say.

My new look was welcomed by a teammate who, until then, had singled-handedly born the burden of "most-likely-to-be-leered-at" Team Canada swimmer. I was taken aback as I never thought myself in the same league –blond with fashion-model cheekbones. "I finally have a partner in crime," she told me. "You're going to get stared at as much as I do. And the funny part is, you have no idea how much you have changed."

A coach once told my mother to be on the lookout for fetishists who attended Paralympic swim meets to photograph amputees. She saw one have his camera confiscated.

I was chosen to model for a Speedo swimsuit calendar where I mixed with able-bodied Olympians who were cultivating their looks for post-Games fame. They were following the lead of 1990s trailblazers such as the U.S. sprinter Florence Griffith Joyner, who glamorized the sport with Hollywood hairstyles, form-fitting track wear and over-the-top nail jobs. Their influence did more to spur my attention to detail than years of pleading by my mom to brush my hair. I underwent media interview training and had stylists for hair and makeup. If the promotion was about tugging at the heartstrings, an amputee athlete might be chosen. If it was about making our sport sexy, it was me and a couple of our hunkier males.

I was flattered by the attention. I understood enough about marketing to realize that different types of athletes appealed to different types of donors.

I was not a promiscuous teen and in hindsight, believe the restrictions placed on me by Team Canada likely saved me from being targeted. Swimming is a sexualized sport – sometimes we change our figure-hugging attire on the deck. While I never experienced it, I was aware of the growing number of athletes coming forward to report sexual harassment. In 1996, Sport Canada initiated safe sport programs that required sports organizations to have harassment policies to qualify for federal funding.

Our disabilities often meant we needed physical attention from a coach, such as a leg stretch or foot massage, on the pool deck. To board the bus without expending my arm strength, a coach might push me by the buttocks. Was that abuse? It might appear to exceed the bounds of acceptable conduct, but I didn't think so at the time nor did my mother, who had me under extraordinary radar.

We all craved normalcy. But for children with disabilities, our normal was unique. Playing practical jokes on each other was part of what bound us, like an unwritten code. We messed with our French-speaking teammates, infecting their vocabularies with the worst of what the English language had to offer.

Some of the pranks involving a teammate's disability went far enough that they wouldn't be tolerated today. But in the 1990s, our camaraderie bound us in a protective shell that might be difficult for outsiders to understand. Our parents, coaches and staff – essentially anyone who was able-bodied – were not welcome in that circle. My mother learned what it was like to be excluded, just as I had been as a child.

***

If Christchurch marked the summit of my personal Everest, Sydney was my chance to celebrate the Sherpa guide who helped get me there. Pepe marvelled at the good fortune of an "old country boy," with an eighth-grade education, cheering on his granddaughter in such a mystical place. "Can you believe this old country boy is here?" he repeated frequently. He was my biggest booster, posting pictures of me on the athletes' shuttle, and my teammates took to calling him Captain Canada. I took pleasure in honouring him. He deserved it. Pepe had been my guardian angel though those painful childhood physio sessions and many life-altering moments en route to the Paralympics.

I spotted Pepe and my parents seated with the Canadian contingent at the opening ceremonies in Stadium Australia, where a crowd of 110,000 gathered to celebrate the nearly 4,000 athletes from 123 countries who would compete at the Games. I nearly came out of my shoes, doing my best kangaroo imitation and screaming like a person possessed. As we paraded in our red-and-white, the realization hit that whether we medalled or not, we were Paralympians – the top of the mountain for disabled athletes. My spirits soared. The joy that had been robbed by MD was now fully resupplied.

My competitors were starting to wonder if my 15-year-old effervescence was a psych-out strategy. Why is she so friendly; is she trying to trick me? The label they placed on me in Christchurch, "Sparkplug of Canada," resurfaced in Sydney. Alternatively, when the moment called for it, "Our Canadian Blond" was employed. When I walked out of the ready room, my name announced and my image cast on a large video board, my coaches must have been tearing their hair out by the amount of energy I spent looking for my parents and Pepe in the stands. In reality, chill Danielle was faster than tense Danielle. I only swam poorly when I was nervous. And my nerves were unimpeachable. Nervousness was limited to the mundane, such as, *Can I get my warmup suit off without falling down on national TV?*

I was the fastest qualifier in the 400 freestyle but finished second in the final. An American edged me by less than a body length. The coaches celebrated my first Paralympic medal, but it had been so long since I lost a race that I was vexed. *Hmm, that's not supposed to happen. Where the fuck did she come from?* It was another lesson in gamesmanship – the American, Lauren Reynolds, had deliberately held back in the qualifying round to conserve energy and feed my overconfidence.

The 400 was my least favourite event and in truth, losing didn't crush my spirit. Just the opposite. I felt rather glib, which played out in the mother of faux pas when we gathered for interviews. I cracked to a reporter in the media pool, *Somebody's gotta drug test that American!*

My coaches were mortified but, thankfully, the reporter realized I was a 15-year-old making an ill-advised but harmless attempt at sarcasm. Thank God we had not reached the social media age with camera phones recording every embarrassing moment.

Lauren, who I had known for a time and considered a friend, grabbed me by the shoulders and said, "Do you realize you just told the entire world that you think I'm on drugs?" *Oh my God, I didn't mean it that way. It was a joke.* We wrote it off as a classic Danielle moment. I was a self-described ditz. In a photo session after the medal ceremony, I encouraged the third-place finisher to join me in kneeling next to Lauren's wheelchair. While my intention was to fit everyone into the frame, the Australian media cast it as an act of incomparable grace. "This is the character of a true champion. This is what Danielle Campo is all about."

Lauren and I had a good laugh over that one. I told her, *I just didn't want you to feel shorter in the picture. How awful would that be? You just won the gold medal. You shouldn't be shorter than the people you beat.*

The episode became part of Danielle Campo folklore and was cited years later when I received the Order of Ontario, the province's highest civilian honour.

Mike, who was coaching me via long-distance phone calls, put a positive spin on the race result. The first quarter of the race marked my fastest ever 100-metre split, he said, boding well for the 100 freestyle final two days away. But while Mike was adept at spinning failure into success, he could also be laughably blunt, like the time later in Sydney when, on the eve of a relay race I was scheduled to anchor, he advised me not to "pull a Maple Leafs" and choke away a big lead, invoking the Toronto NHL team that so often disappoints its fans.

My dad helped hit a reset button after the 400. "It's OK," he said. "Go back to the village and refocus. We came for gold. Go back and refocus on the reason we came." A teammate who overheard the conversation was horrified that my parents would put so much pressure on me, to which I replied, *Screw that. I need the pressure.*

Two days later I returned to the Sydney Olympic Park Aquatic Centre, its 10,000 seats jammed with schoolchildren bused in to ensure a full house, intent on obliterating the field in the 100. *I'm so close,* I thought, *I can actually be a Paralympic gold medallist.* I was no longer an unknown commodity, and in fact was heavily favoured in my remaining races. All those hours perfecting my left-footed takeoff and turn techniques paid off. Instead of trailing at the turn, my traditional Achille's heel, I was even with my chief competitors. Then I pulled away and with 30 metres left, was a body-length ahead. My only risk was celebrating too fast, only to choke on a mouthful of water and sink one metre short of the finish – another Danielle moment.

My face hurt from the emotional explosion of touching first, two body lengths ahead of the silver medallist. I saw a Paralympic Games volunteer weeping and even the reporters were jumping up and down. I heard my mother screaming in a rapturous celebration. My dad, oddly, was nowhere to be seen. I was disbelieving. Was he out having a pee when I won my first gold? After all that finishing-second-means-your-didn't-finish-first shit? *It can't be!* I learned later that in a pratfall captured live by the CBC cameras, he put new meaning in the expression blown away – in fact, he passed out. Fell flat on his face. A Japanese fan was seen tending to him on the floor.

I would never again swim two lengths of an Olympic pool in one minute, 14 seconds, a world record that stood for 12 years.

In the media bay, the first thing out of my mouth was an apology for my ill-advised joke about drug testing Lauren Reynolds, which sent the reporters into fits of laughter. An American journalist was quick to reassure me. "We all love you Danielle. You could probably tell us you murdered someone and we would laugh."

I thought winning my first international gold medal in Christchurch was the ultimate fuck you to my painful childhood, but watching the Maple Leaf climb that flagpole in Sydney, serenaded by O Canada, and with my family in the stands, was how I imagine Neil Armstrong feeling when he stepped off that lunar module.

"Winner of the gold medal, representing Canada, Danielle Campo."

Walking to the podium to collect my medal gave me the sensation of a roller-coaster ride; each step the click-click-click of the coaster's slow climb to the top. The Canadian flag reaching its apex was the bone-shaking adrenalin rush of the coaster's descent.

I struggled to remember which side of my chest to cover with my hand, a show of respect encouraged by my mom, opting instead for the hands-behind-the-back, uber-cool technique of Joanne Millar, a Canadian Olympian I admired. Clenching my medallist bouquet and feeling the weight of the medal around my neck, I sang parts of the anthem but was struggling to contain my emotions, determined to avoid a televised ugly-cry. Pepe, whom I could see along with my parents, had lost that battle. His shoulders shook as tears cascaded down his weathered cheeks.

In that moment I knew what must be done: *I will give the flowers to Pepe.*

I found him in the seats, got as close as I could and flung the bouquet his way, yelling out not to lose the specially designed pin that was attached.

"I'll just hold them for you," he would later say. But I was not getting them back. Carrying a medallist bouquet told the world that you were connected to someone special. Before Sydney was done, Pepe's colourful collection was bountiful, thanks to three gold medals and a silver. The flower exchange was the start of a tradition that would last through the remainder of Sydney and on to the Athens Games in 2004.

By the time the 50-metre freestyle arrived, I was so heavily favoured that I allowed myself to imagine the infamous parties that beckoned at the end of the Games, and how I would stage-manage the race to get my close friend, Australia's Amanda Fraser, on the podium as a second- or third-place finisher.

Amanda was a national hero, but in me, the Australian media found a rare champion who combined skill, looks and charisma – the "Sparkplug of Canada." They openly mused about making the outgoing Canadian an honorary Aussie. I was oblivious to their adulation. I was thinking about Amanda.

When I touched the wall with more than a body-length lead, the first words out of my mouth were directed at her. *What did you get?* I screamed. She would join me on the podium as bronze medallist.

When the events wrapped up, with Canada topping the medal count, we returned to the Canadian village to find it stocked to the rafters with Molson Canadian beer. We started a bonfire in the street and when the Aussie firefighters arrived, it wasn't to douse the blaze but to feed it with wooden pallets. Drinking alcohol at age 15 was a rite of passage, I was told, as long as I stayed put in the village. Once teammates debunked a myth that my mother had planted – that I could be kicked off the team if a blood test detected alcohol – I happily partook.

By the second night I needed a break. When a team manager saw me dumping my third beer into the ground and replacing it with water, she observed: "That's how I know you are going to be OK in life. Very strategic."

Since, unlike the boys, I was forbidden from leaving the complex to party in downtown Sydney, I invited my American and Australian friends to our village. The Sparkplug of Canada, it turns out, applied to both the pool and the party.

After three days of booze-filled celebrations, we wrapped ourselves in the Sydney2000 bedspreads that served as our parting gifts and waited at the airport for our flight home. I was so exhausted that my teammates scooped me up in the blanket and carried me to the gate.

Recognizing my alcohol-diminished state, Mom said, "This is the only time, no questions asked. Got it?" Be careful with your image, she said, so you will never be forced to rebuild it. "Don't ever do anything that takes away from all of the great things you've done."

Mom's advice, as always, was spot on.

My packaging as a wholesome, salable, Paralympic commodity escalated after Sydney as Swimming Canada sought to grow its fan base. In my hometown, opportunity knocked for a newly minted local celebrity. Swimming Canada managed the national gigs and my mother the local side-hustles. My 16th birthday was spent at a six-hour magazine photoshoot. If a promotion called for a brilliant smile and a strawberry blond, I was dispatched to the beauty salon. I worked with sponsors ranging from a car dealership to clothing and sunglass distributors, a trucking company and not-for-profits such as Muscular Dystrophy Canada, which often paired me with firefighters, a major source of their fundraising.

My conduct was carefully controlled, with coaches warning me against brand-killing acts such as drinking alcohol in public. Not because I was underage, but because of the harm it would do their brand. It was left to my mom to add, "And *because* you are underage!" I went from my parents calling the shots to Swimming Canada saying, "Curfew's at 9."

With our pet retriever Boomer

Receiving my silver Sunfire from Jim and Gus Revenberg   *Modelling my Sydney medals*

When, at 15, the Gus Revenberg Chevrolet dealership offered me four years with a car of my choosing, my dad was mortified when I picked a compact Sunfire over a Monte Carlo. *But the Sunfire is so cute,* I said in my defence, still too young to drive but happy to hang out with friends in the driveway huddled around the car stereo.

If my Christchurch homecoming was the Tragically Hip at Massey Hall, Sydney was the Beatles at Shea Stadium. A huge crowd and crush of media greeted me at the airport, and 1,500 cheering students gathered in the St. Anne gymnasium for a welcome-home assembly in which the gifting of my silver Sunfire was re-enacted.

I may have been a gold medallist, but I remained a 15-year-old 10th grader with a disability, still trying to find my way in the able-bodied world. When I walked into the auditorium wearing my podium suit, my medals still clanked and my pant legs still swished. I still found being paraded in front of the school population mortifying, which was odd considering how well I had taken to the adulation of Sydney and Christchurch. I'm a rock star to my schoolmates, I thought cynically, because the assembly got them out of classes. But one undeniable positive emerged from that embarrassment – I would never again be asked to explain my funny walk. Suddenly I had an identity: Danielle Campo, Paralympic swimmer.

I began to enjoy universal acceptance from the student cliques, attended several proms – including one with a future cardiovascular surgeon with whom I would cross paths in adulthood – and was granted entry to the booth where the Grade 12s piped top 40's music into the cafeteria, where only the coolest kids were allowed.

There was a certain mystique attached to my many prolonged absences, to training camps in Montreal or Calgary, the hub of the Canadian Olympic community, and international meets in Berlin, Nice, Strasbourg and the 2002 IPC World Championships in Mar del Plata, Argentina, where I won two golds and a silver and was exposed to a country still recovering from years of political unrest. Teachers afforded me the same preferential treatment as the junior hockey players who almost never attended class. Thank God for the patient tutors who kept me academically afloat.

Royally Flushed

The 2002 Commonwealth Games in Manchester, England, marked the first time disabled swimmers were invited. I was among four Canadians in a field of 24 from the 72 Commonwealth countries. In a field that included swimmers from all classifications, I won bronze in my only race, the 50 freestyle. This prompted my parents to remark with sarcasm that they travelled all the way to England to watch a 34-second splash and dash that I didn't win.

I was one of two Canadians to attend a private audience with Queen Elizabeth II which, given my faux pas in Sydney about drug testing the American swimmer, struck me as odd. *Do they want me to get us in trouble?* I was old enough to understand the significance of representing Canada before the Monarch, but still too young to harness my impetuousness.

She was so approachable – a soft-spoken little grandma with kick-ass, pastel-coloured clothes and flawless skin, the product, I assumed, of bathing in Rubies cosmetic products. After delivering my scripted greetings on behalf of Canada, I did the Danielle thing – forget what they taught me in etiquette training and wing it. Like most teenage girls at the time, the Royals I really cared about were Diana's sons William and Harry. Who better to ask than their grandmother?

I curtsied and fixed her in my gaze.

May I ask you the question I really want to know?

"Of course, darling."

Where are your grandsons?

The Queen laughed, replying, "Well, like most teenage boys, they are probably still sleeping."

She privately told aides about how refreshing it was to have an unscripted conversation with a real person. When our paths crossed again, at a Golden Jubilee reception in Toronto where I was accompanied by my mom, the Queen picked me out of a crowd and walked my way, extending her hand. "Ah. There is my favourite Canadian swimmer," she said, causing my mother to nearly pass out.

I restrained an impulse to reach out and hug her.

Still no grandsons with you? I said.

"I know," she replied. "One day they'll come."

My second star-struck moment in Manchester involved a member of swimming's royalty. It happened after a coach coaxed me into the warmup pool, which I had resisted because of the intimidating – and very large – able-bodied swimmers who occupied it. I considered it a shark tank.

Swimming my laps, one of the monsters approaching from behind grabbed my foot and squeezed it, which I assumed was the able-bodied way of saying move aside, I'm coming through. (Paras tap the foot before passing). When I tore off my goggles to confront him, the hulking young man was apologetic. I was mortified to learn it was Ian Thorpe, aka the Thorpedo, Australia's most decorated Olympian, the fastest swimmer on the planet, tall and lean with short-cropped hair, deep tan wrapped in a black Fastskin body suit and a smile the size of Queensland. Hunk City. I had to stop myself from swooning.

"Sorry mate, I didn't see you. I thought I was going to run you right over," he said, then, with a quizzical look, added, "I've heard about you. You're the crazy Canadian. Everyone's talking about how fun you are."

Later we hung out in the cafeteria, joking about the encounter, and remain in contact to this day. That he knew me by reputation was mind-boggling. He confessed to mistaking the idle legs of my swimming technique with an unorthodox training drill. But the Thorpedo wasn't gunning for me romantically. Twelve years later he came out as gay, confessing to the torment of cloaking his sexuality to preserve his image as an Olympic stud. I knew his secret. Everyone in swimming did. But to the outside world, he was the most eligible bachelor in Oz.

Asked in a media scrum my favourite part of the Games, I replied, *Getting touched by Ian Thorpe.* Between my unscripted comments to the Queen and the Thorpe gushing, my Swimming Canada handlers concluded I would need more media training.

Sadly, Manchester also opened my eyes to the warts of international swimming. Mixing for the first time with Olympic athletes illuminated how much better they were treated than Paralympians. I received 14 bathing suits, three pairs of running shoes, 27 bathing caps and 12 sets of goggles – for a single race. By comparison, in the Sydney Paralympics I received one suit for each of the four events I entered.

Bigger sponsors. More media attention. Better food. Grander ceremonies. The Paralympics weren't popular enough to compete.

Olympians dwelled in what I considered a cutthroat world, from their bountiful kit to the minions who tended to their every whim, the laptops and other high-tech gadgetry they were supplied, massage therapists 24/7 and the animosity they harbored for opponents and teammates alike. I saw them quibble over time allotted with favored coaches. I saw them caught up in doping scandals. Even the partying was Olympian.

One night, the four Paralympic swimmers representing Canada took stock of their Olympic counterparts and concluded, "Thank God we are disabled. This world sucks." The able-bodied athletes clearly craved our camaraderie. Carrying your teammate's duffel bag to an event, as we often did, was foreign to them.

The disparity between the two worlds weighed on me. And worse, in my eyes, the Paralympic movement was starting to take on Olympic attributes.

In Sydney, countries thought nothing of filing formal challenges to an athlete's disability classification, for a $1,000 fee, hoping to have their results voided by proving they were not as disabled as they claimed. Since the process could involve a physio test, some did it to fatigue a rival before a race. Once, a rival country threatened to challenge mine. My coaches suspected it was a ploy to tire me. They argued, with documented evidence, that my swimming classification claimed less of a disability then my dry-land classification. The challenge never went through.

Random drug testing was an ever-present threat – and teams exploited it. Coaches had us place our water bottles next to a Canadian lane supervisor to prevent rivals from spiking them with banned substances. My naivete made this difficult to believe. *Would someone actually do this to my water?* "They would if they wanted to win the gold medal," a coach said. Many countries had started to pay athletes for winning medals. The spectre of a good friend in the next lane slipping me stanozolol, the performance enhancing steroid that sank Canadian sprinter Ben Johnson, or a rival yanking on my bad leg in the warmup pool, became a cold reality. It saddened me that this blight had infected our previously sacrosanct world.

I was sent home from Manchester before the after-parties because the coaches feared I would be set upon. "Thank God you went home early," my teammate Benoit Huot said, "because it was one giant orgy."

When I left England, swimming no longer felt like a family affair – teammates and adversaries alike giving the middle finger to their disabilities. Maybe, after five years of hardcore competition, I was losing my ability to look the other way. The Sparkplug of Canada was burning out but, having made no plans for the post-pool world, she could not swim away.

I enrolled in child and youth worker classes at Mohawk College in Hamilton and swam with the McMaster University varsity team, which accommodated Paralympians, but I was not posting good enough times to challenge the podium at the 2004 Paralympics. Faced with the choice of retiring or committing fully to the Athens Games, I packed for the National Training Centre in Calgary, where I lived with my old coach Scott, now a member of the national coaching staff, and his wife. It put me in the company of Olympic-bound athletes, who were rock stars in the Calgary party scene.

The town was enraptured by the Calgary Flames' run to the Stanley Cup finals, and if I didn't score tickets to the Saddledome, I was a regular at outdoor watch-parties on the Red Mile. Drafted by the Flames, my old swimming partner Ryan Donally came on the scene, and now I was hanging out with hockey royalty too. When I missed a Saturday practice after staying out late the night before, Scott made me do laps until I nearly vomited.

Captivated by the good times, heightened freedom and Rocky Mountain vistas, once again I told my mother I wasn't coming home.

"Yes you are," she said. "The mountains may be beautiful but they don't love you back."

At 19, I had never held a full-time job, relying instead on my Swimming Canada stipends, which had grown to $2,200 a month, the odd sponsorship and my parents' generosity. I applied to a Gap clothing store in Calgary, worked a training shift on the sales floor, stocked shelves and hated it. After two shifts, I quit.

My coaches, including Scott, discouraged me from working, which was great for swimming but not for life after the pool. Sarcastically I thought, *Yes Danielle, this will prepare you for the working world.*

What swimming did introduce me to was the global scene, even if I didn't heed my mother's advice to attend mass on foreign soils. At the worlds in Argentina, while our team was mostly shielded from the political and economic strife tearing at the country, I saw enough poverty to know that Canada is a privileged place to live. The modest amounts we spent on local clothing caused a shopkeeper to weep for joy since she would be able to stay open until month's end.

Our translator made it known he would stuff himself in our suitcases to get out of the country. A passerby on the beach told us to hide our iPods, warning we would most certainly be robbed. My mother endured long lineups to withdraw cash from a bank and required an escort back to her hotel.

When I qualified for Athens 2004, Team Canada held its training camp in Kos, one of Greece's Dodecanese islands known for its sandy beaches and the 15th Century Neratzia Castle. One day, my teammates and I decided it would be fun to swim the Aegean Sea to the Turkish mainland four km away. Dumb idea. We were turned back at gunpoint by the coast guard.

Daredevil adventures aside, the carefree 13-year-old from Christchurch was gone. In her place was a diva in the making who threw a hissy fit because her luggage was five days late arriving. I fretted over whether I still had the goods to hold off a wave of younger swimmers, including the speedy persons with short stature who, for the first time, were included in the S7 category of the Paralympics. While physically I was in the best shape of my life, mentally I was starting to flounder. The results showed. While I was the reigning gold medallist and world record holder, I finished fourth in the 100 freestyle. It was my first time missing the podium in international competitions involving my specialty races.

I thought: *Wow, this is shitty.* The media doesn't talk to you when you finish fourth. Sympathy replaces adulation. Even the commentators appeared disappointed.

In the 400 final, the fear of leaving the Games without a medal gripped me. Winning used to come naturally. Now it was the fight of a lifetime, where every stroke, every breath, could be the difference between the podium and a pat on the back. I felt like the swimming equivalent of being on life support, which would play a vital role in my brush with death 17 years later.

I summoned every ounce of strength, every time-shaving trick in the book, to touch third. With the weight of medalling off my back, I won bronze in the 50 and silver in the freestyle relay, where I had been relieved of my anchor position because another swimmer posted better times.

Two bronze and a silver didn't live up to the "Tecumseh's Golden Girl" banners displayed throughout my hometown. I returned to a muted reception at the airport with a smattering of media. Now graduated from high school, there was no assembly. I was not aligned with a local swim club to offer a cheering section. Many of my friends had left town for school. The air was out of my Paralympic balloon. If you are no longer a winner, even the marketing department loses interest.

Still receiving Swimming Canada subsidies, I trained for two more years in London, Ont., where I studied to complete my child and youth worker diploma. I had my first serious boyfriend and volunteered with Muscular Dystrophy Canada. And after all those years of happily attending swim practice, absorbing the advice of my coaches, modifying my stroke and my physique, I could no longer find the passion.

And at a nondescript meet in Portland, Ore., having finished college, I told the coaches that I had hit my wall. I was finished. Even the taste of pool water repulsed me. Unlike how I had pictured my retirement, my parents were not in the stands and Pepe was nowhere to be seen. I said goodbye to the sport that put Ditch Danielle in my wake.

***

Somewhere between hopscotching the globe in Team Canada attire and reporting for my first full-time job, I lost my identity. I thought:

I will never again be the best in the world at something.

I will sit in a cubicle for the next 30 years, grinding out paychecks instead of collecting government stipends.

I won't appear in newspapers and on TV.

I won't celebrate with my teammates.

I won't march in opening ceremonies

I won't carry a flag.

I won't hear my national anthem played for me.

Like most Olympians, I often toyed with the idea of making a comeback, only to change my mind once training resumed. I'm an adrenalin junkie, down for the thrill of competing but not for the work it took to win.

For the first time in my life, I had to buy my own sunglasses and bathing suits. The four years free use of my Sunfire ran out. Dad handed me $8,000 for a new car, but when he told me I would have to pay him back, I was dumbfounded. I earned a degree but, so what, everyone else had one too.

When I threatened, repeatedly, to move to Australia, Mom invoked the 24-hour rule: "Wait 24 hour before you make a decision like that." I always recanted.

Given my brief history at the Gap, it should have come as no surprise that I struggled in the working world. In my first full-time job, as a residential support worker with the Children's Aid Society, I helped foster parents care for children who had been removed from troubled households. I couldn't have ventured further from the pampered life of a carded Canadian swimmer. One day, my supervisor set me straight when I told her I was going home for a nap.

"Are you not feeling well?"

No, I just need a nap.

"It doesn't work that way Danielle. You can't just go home for a nap. If you are sick, you can go home. Or if you are taking vacation time."

No, I just need a nap.

I struggled with basic employee relations concepts such as time sheets and flex hours. Preparing case reports was a challenge. My supervisor sat me down one day and said, "Think of me as your coach. And you're the swimmer. When your coach told you what to do, you did it. When I tell you how to do something, you do it. Your case reports are your new Olympics. I want the best written reports and best notes that you can produce from each family."

I was like a recent arrival from Mars, aka, competitive swimming. Framing it that way made sense to me. While I often started the day wondering what I had gotten myself into, I came to be good at it. I found ways to pierce through what was troubling the children and develop plans to make them happier.

In a reversal, drawing upon the pain of my childhood, I became *their* coach. I identified their gaps and deficiencies. I developed the counselling equivalent of training regimens, focusing on what worked in them, not what was broken, just as I had been trained to do as a disabled athlete. I like to think I taught them to breathe.

And I treated the parents whose children had been taken away with dignity and respect. Many didn't know how to react if I asked their opinion. One dad told me he had never been hugged, not even in childhood – no wonder he didn't know how to raise his kids. "No one ever looked me in the eyes and talked to me," he said. "You're the only one who ever treated me like a human."

We've all had struggles, I would say.

Having finished my social work degree at the University of Windsor, I took on the position of family service worker, performing the profoundly unhappy task of removing children from unhealthy home environments. I took a three-year-old boy from his mother, two days before Christmas. The home was a hornet's nest of substance and spousal abuse. Taking that boy broke my heart, but it was the right thing to do.

I saw promise in the mom, but she needed help. One day I asked her to hold a mirror to her face, as if to confront her demons for the sake of her child. When she asked what I saw in the mirror, I said a survivor and fighter who was going to deservedly regain custody of her son. Years later, when I was confronting serious health issues, she reminded me of the gesture, saying, "Now I'm pointing the mirror at you, and you must survive." Sadly, she was never reunited with her son.

I was assigned to the night watch with a teenager with a history of harming herself and CAS staff. We had long, emotional conversations and I shared some of my history. She warmed to me, and on my third shift said, "I'm not gonna hit you over the head with a cookie sheet. I'm not going to throw you down the stairs or hurt you. I could really, really hurt you if I did that. But you're cool. You talk to me, and you treat me with respect. So I'm not going to hurt you."

Thanks, I replied. *Please let me know if that ever changes.*

Sadly, her demons were too strong for our safety net. At her funeral, and with Mom at my side, her grandmother approached me and said, "She always talked about how you treated her with respect." Mom said it was her proudest moment.

In another case, I followed a tip that an infant was being raised in a home frequented by drug traffickers. During the home inspection, I heard a gunshot ring out two floors below, shattering a window in the basement apartment. A dealer had come to settle a score with his buyer, who lived there.

A drug enforcement team had been surveilling the house. When they heard the shot, a group of armed-to-the-teeth cops burst through the door, ordering us to get down on the floor. The last thing they expected was a CAS worker holding a baby. I fumbled for my badge, only to be shooed out the door carrying a screaming child in a blanket. I called my family to assure them the CAS worker on the news was safe, but the bad guys were in custody. My brother Kenny, who had joined the police force, said: "You need to get a new job."

My mother said, and it became my motto: "They may never remember your name, but they'll always remember the way you made them feel." I was adept at breaking down the barriers put up by parents who felt disrespected by the system and approached my help with skepticism, needing reassurance that my offer to bring coffee did not come with a catch. I tried to treat them compassionately, knowing that had it not been for my family, or under slightly different circumstances, I could be walking in their shoes. Supporting the people who needed it, and responded to it, kept me going.

I was assigned the file of a motorcycle gang member where it was suspected children were in an unsafe environment. He wanted my help with a recovery plan to get them back. We worked on the plan over the triple-triple Tim Hortons coffees I brought him. He didn't get his kids back but we stayed on good terms. When another parent on the CAS radar made overtures to me that I took as threatening, my biker buddy interceded and the threats stopped.

He said: "All is good now Danielle."

I became an in-demand social worker with a waiting list of parents who requested me by name. But those moments of fulfilment were becoming scarce. I was conflicted over the rights of parents versus the obligation of the CAS to protect children. The impossible tasks, like taking newborns away from their moms in the maternity ward because they were on our watch list – which was the case with the dad who threatened me – weighed heavily. That case drove me to tears. When the nurses caught me taking a circuitous route around their station to conceal my weeping, I realized it was time, once again, to reinvent myself.

When I returned from Sydney2000, I volunteered for Muscular Dystrophy Canada and became their national ambassador. I was invited to a conference to share my story, and the one I delivered was unvarnished: Yes, I triumphed. No, it wasn't easy. My unscripted, raw-and-real account struck a chord with the firefighters who had been supporting MD since 1954, raising more than $100 million in their Fill the Boot campaigns. They helped purchase wheelchairs, hospital beds, leg braces, walkers, respirators, and other life-changing equipment. They supported research and advocacy.

In me, they found a champion who had literally, if not wobblily, walked the walk. My mother and I travelled the country sharing our story. Once, when driving through Ontario cottage country, we both wept when we came upon a "boot toll," where firefighters lined the roadside collecting donations for MD. We pulled over to thank them. They marvelled at being visited by "the girl on the poster."

For a time, I trained in Chatham with an obscenely early start time of 4 a.m. Mom would drive me and then curl up in the parking lot to sleep for the two hours. It was near a fire hall and the firefighters brought her coffee for the drive home.

I often addressed school children, my seven medals in tow. Years later I was contacted by a woman whose class I addressed when she was in Grade 4. She told me I had inspired her to pursue competitive sports. She took up wrestling, and medalled at the 2022 world championships.

Mom and I worked alongside inspiring fundraisers such as Launie Fletcher, district chief of the Coldstream Fire Station in Middlesex County, whose golf tournament raised more than $330,000 for MD in 13 years. They

Here's an engagement photo from my first marriage, which in hindsight was an ill-fated checklist item

became family.

When I left the CAS, I found my dream job as director of programs and services with Muscular Dystrophy Canada, which put me in direct contact with my kindred spirits with MD. My job was to ensure our programs met their needs. I specialized in dispute resolution – with applicants who didn't get the funding they wanted and with disgruntled staff. Compared to the CAS, it was a walk in the park. Later I served as director of people and culture, educating staff on how to interact with MD families and work with medical personnel.

Joining the MDC staff brought me full circle, allowing me to stay grounded, give thanks and pay forward the kindnesses I had received.

You Know He's a Keeper When...

My first marriage was a Kardashian moment. You know, try it on like an expensive shoe, discard it if you don't own a matching purse. I will call him Vlad and say that his family emigrated from Eastern Europe when he was in grade school. He was a first responder and we were set up by a mutual friend. Tall with carefully groomed black hair and liberal with his cologne, a techno music and MMA fan, he was kind and thoughtful during our courtship, bringing flowers to my workplace each Friday. My brothers, half-mockingly and with exaggerated swoons, would harken the arrival of "Smella's White Knight."

Marrying Vlad now strikes me as a checklist item in the manufactured image of Paralympic Danielle. At 25, it was what the instruction manual said I was supposed to do. We dated for 18 months, were engaged for six and wed in a Roman Catholic ceremony. In the context of my muscular dystrophy, it represented a gold medal for normalcy – *yes, I can find a guy and live the dream.*

Not long after we said our vows, the dream fell apart. He was cynical, thinking the world was out to get him. He played the poor-me card. He was not a big fan of career women, preferring me home to cook dinner. He thought I spent too much time with my family. He doted on me, and not in a good way. It angered him if I did the most menial task, prompting me to wait until he had left for work before putting away the Christmas tree. If it's possible to make someone feel *more* disabled by constantly doing things for them, he was accomplishing it.

The tipping point came when he forbade me from travelling to Muscular Dystrophy Association of Canada conferences because he didn't want me hanging out with firefighters, our largest fundraisers. Although I never gave him a reason to doubt my fidelity, he had been cheated on and thought them a threat.

He was putting my light out.

I became vindictive and mean, looking for any opportunity to thwart his control. One day I found one, of all places, in the kitchen. He and his brother were on the paleo diet of lean meats, fish, fruits, vegetables, nuts and seeds. They were avoiding rich dishes that they claimed were causing stomach problems. One night, I cooed about preparing a lovely chicken wing dinner the way he had asked, using coconut flower, when in fact I had slammed those wings with enough butter and breadcrumbs to choke a drainpipe. I could barely contain myself as they gleefully scarfed them down. Their much-ballyhooed adverse reaction never happened. It was beautiful.

My mother at first cautioned me about the travails of the first year of marriage, then realized that her daughter was profoundly, irreversibly unhappy. It was only in Vlad's absence did she see the "real Danielle" return. On our way home from a muscular dystrophy event, she said, "You look grey. Something's not right. I need to know what's going on." When I described how much he had changed since the wedding – how he was already laying out a militaristic approach to raising our kids – she said, "That's not a marriage. That's not compromising. It's certainly not love."

My dad tried to move Vlad away from his old-world approach, without luck. It was all I could do to keep Craig and Kenny from paying him a visit with darker intentions. *You're a police officer Kenny; not a good look.*

Encouraged by my mother, we decided to take one last stab at saving our marriage with a couples' vacation to Ormand Beach, Fla. "Sometimes when you get out of the city and you get out of normal day, everyday life, you'll get there and you'll be like, oh, there are things still here," Mom, in counsellor mode, said. "There are lifelines that we can work on."

Within minutes of landing, we were arguing again, over something so trivial that I think it involved Tater Tots. I wanted to strangle him with that lifeline. We were done.

Dennis McLeod was at the resort in Ormand Beach, too. I didn't know him but we had mutual friends who gathered in Florida on week 38 of the time-share calendar. One morning we were hanging out by the pool when he walked out, shirtless and tattooed, wearing a black bathing suit. He was fine featured in the manner of Colin Farrell and had what a certain generation would call bedroom eyes. I was in the swimming pool and couldn't help noticing his physique, the product of a pushup-and-crunch regimen he had been following for six months. A voice in my head said, *He's hot but your're married. Chill, Danielle.* As if to hit a reset button on my libido, I dunked my head underwater and came up cleansed of impure thoughts.

It wasn't his six-pack but his smile that I found most attractive. It was a joyful smile, a smile of someone who liked to live large, and to a woman in an unhappy marriage, her partner perpetually ill-tempered and her joy stolen by muscular dystrophy, it was pure sunshine.

His friends summoned him over to commiserate on their hangovers from the previous night's bar hopping in Ormand Beach. It was not yet noon, but in Canadian fashion they were mixing bloody Caesars – vodka, clamato juice and tabasco sauce – for a morning-after healer. A friend introduced us. Denny smiled and said hi.

We started chatting by the pool and later at the beach. He addressed me in a measured, even tone, soft-spoken, as if every word mattered. There might have been a touch of Pepe in him. He told me he was divorced, with two kids, and wanted to be a firefighter, which is either the greatest pickup line in history or the real deal. It appealed to me since these heroes support muscular dystrophy with their boot campaigns.

A young girl in our party wanted to play in the ocean. So did I, but no one else put up their hand except Denny. Off we went, but I had difficulty staying upright as the waves crashed against my unstable legs. Each time I tumbled to the ocean floor, Denny helped me up. We joked about him getting an early start on his rescuer career. I spent more time under the water than above it. As salt water and mucus gushed out of my nose and mouth, I was overcome by the wonder of the sea, crying out, *This is amazing!* To which Denny laughed, "It doesn't look like it's fun for you. But if you say so..."

Under the circumstances, with me tossing about in the water like a dead mackerel, it was an odd time for Denny to notice the Sydney 2000 tattoo on my left shoulder and connect me to that Paralympic gold medallist and world champion swimmer he heard about. A menacing looking fish passed by and Denny recalled seeing a shark that last time he was here. Miraculously, my mastery of the water returned and I was no longer nautically challenged. I beat him to the shore.

When we returned to the group he approached my husband, saying, "I have your wife's boob in my pocket." The waves had jarred the padding from my top and it landed in the water. Vlad was indifferent. Everyone laughed and a breezy vibe developed between our merged friend groups. We found ourselves at the same bar most nights with Denny often occupying a chair near mine. We spent more time playing in the surf. We talked for what seemed like hours. It was innocent, strictly best-buddy territory, and only in hindsight did we realize the spark of attraction.

I was sure by then that my marriage was over, but I wasn't coming home with a new boyfriend. No, I was far from ready for that. But if Vlad had been the checklist item for Paralympic Danielle, Denny was the embodiment of hope – hope that a gallant, spontaneous, livin'-large kind of guy like him could come my way. This man would be both my protector and my ignition switch. He would give space but call me out when I fucked up. He would *not* make me feel more disabled. I swore I would never date again, but if I did, I would look for a partner like Denny McLeod.

We realized months later that Denny was on the same wavelength, telling his mother, "I gotta find a girl like her."

I gave him my phone number with the offer to help open doors in his career through my connections with the firefighters. By the time he followed up, six months later, I was single.

Unwinding my marriage would be a test of my parents' faith, and it took a stroke of good fortune to get there. I was serving as sponsor for my sister-in-law Tricia's conversion to Catholicism, called the Rite of Christian Initiation of Adults, when we took a class that involved charting your lifeline from cradle to current state. When mine was finished, Tricia looked at me with a quizzical expression, like I had omitted my birth. "So, you're married, right? You forgot to put that in your lifeline."

Oh, crap. Now I had to bring Tricia into my circle of trust about the marriage trouble. She was joined by a woman involved in the RCIA program, who had known me since my teens and took note of my unhappiness. "There's something going on with you," she said, "and I can't put my finger on it." With their help we engaged the priest in a discussion about annulment, which allows RCs to end their marriage without being barred from the sacraments. An annulment means that, in the eyes of the church, your marriage never happened.

The priest advised marriage counselling, which failed miserably. After one session, when the counsellor had me alone, she said, "You need to leave." *Pardon me?* "The writing is on the wall that these behaviours are starting like this, and I'm afraid they're going to escalate into something bigger. I've seen it a thousand times. This isn't going to end well. You gotta go."

As deep-rooted as their RC beliefs were, my parents did not stand in my way. The priest told them I had grounds for an annulment, and that was good enough. They understood the deep abyss in which I had landed. When I told them I couldn't wait for the drawn-out annulment process, they supported my decision to file for divorce. Never have I so valued their love and support.

Leaving Vlad required a safety plan that was as carefully orchestrated as a swim meet. One day, when he was at work, I packed a bag and drove to my parents' house. I pulled into my old spot in the driveway, cut the engine and exhaled. I mean, a long, slow release of breath. *Hawwwwwww.* A lawyer served Vlad with divorce papers and told him that if he wanted to reach me, he had to do it through my parents.

While I never regretted the decision, moving back into my childhood bedroom felt like a failure. Danielle Campo was no failure. But before I could move on, I had to let loose. My first six months as a divorced woman were spent in a booze-infused time warp. It was like I travelled back to my late teens in the party and bar-hopping scene that started in Manchester, except now, I had a full-time job to support my cavorting. We booked rooms at the Caesars Windsor casino hotel to crash without answering to our parents.

I was oblivious to the playboys who put me on their radar, but Denny, who was also frequenting the downtown, wasn't. When we ran into each other, he took advantage of his chance to serve as my protector. My girlfriends and I made for a striking trio, and we had no difficulty getting guys to either share, or completely surrender, their tables. One night Denny arrived at the Kildare House, an Irish pub, to find me, coincidentally, at a table filled with his friends. He was impressed and attracted, by my assertiveness. It seemed like fate was propelling us to a common landing spot.

For a time, and because I was still getting over my breakup, hanging out in group settings was good enough. It didn't seem that we were dating. Both scarred by our last relationships, Denny the victim of infidelity and me of an obscene mismatch, we were going so slowly that describing it as platonic would be like saying Vesuvius was a campfire. Our first date, to a Muse concert at Joe Louis Arena in Detroit, offered a sign that we were star-crossed: Denny had injured his knee playing football, which made navigating the arena steps harder on him than me. We both limped our way to the seats and back. He limped to the concession stand to fetch me beer.

I was attracted to his calm and empathy, which he gave unconditionally. Today they call it "holding space." He was attracted to my fire. Both arms now adorned with half-sleeve tattoos, he could lean toward the rock 'n' roller's shoulder length mane but would shave his head if it meant convincing his kids to get haircuts. He was a patient, kind and even-keeled dad.

Years earlier, Denny was building a career as a vehicle designer with Porsche, and later Magna Steyr, in Michigan, when his second child Ella was born. He quit because the daily commute was costing him time with his kids. He took a job as IT co-ordinator for the Windsor Essex Community Heath Centre, which operates a network of medical offices in the region. Then he moved to Green Shield Canada, a not-for-profit benefits carrier. He parked his passion for cars at the side of the road.

His dating strike-zone was music, particularly obscure bands in small venues. If you want to date Denny McLeod, you had better like the Alabama Shakes. He awakened me to the alternative music scene, far removed from the boy-band era where I was raised but in later years regarded as shallow. Give me the Tragically Hip over the Backstreet Boys, any day, I would tell our coaches at swim practice. The first year we dated, Denny and I saw a dozen concerts as the alt scene pulled me further from the mainstream and my carefully curated image as Paralympic Danielle. It felt like a cool, fresh breeze. Like freedom.

On a trip to Las Vegas to see the Scottish rock band Biffy Clyro, we stopped to get tattoos after Denny's web surfing found a highly rated Vegas artist. My tat was the Athens 2004 Olympic logo, to go along with the Sydney 2000 ink already on my shoulder. Denny got symbols representing his children – a dove for Calum and a fairy for Ella. The front-row seats that we scored due to my disability were great for sightlines, but not so for newly needled tattoos. It hurt like hell when the crowd moshed forward. Ouch … yeah! … ouch … yeah! Luckily, I had Denny to shield me.

He was winning me over to his counterculture world. It was so unlike the carefully curated image of the infallible Olympic athlete, but no less exhilarating.

On a whim, we applied to be contestants on the maiden season of Amazing Race Canada, the reality show where travellers crisscross the globe in a test of problem-solving skills. We were on track to join the show when Denny realized he couldn't be away from his children for 30 days.

By the third date we were talking about kids. I told him that if he didn't see at least one child in our future, it's off to the friend zone. *I want more,* I said. *I want to have a baby.* He rolled his eyes and said with a sarcastic lilt, "It's gonna take a special woman…" He was nine years my senior and had done his share of school Christmas concerts. But the courtship rolled on.

Leery from my last romance and a divorced man entering my life, Mom, a bereavement specialist at the Canadian Mental Health Association, asked her friends and contacts if they knew him. In Windsor, the circles are small. The reviews were stunningly consistent. The sacrifices he had made for his children were commonly known. "Oh my God, he is the nicest guy."

Spontaneity. Adventure. Fun. Trust. Those were the bedrocks of our relationship. One day, grabbing a beer in a pub after watching his son play in a

59

Denny and I thrive on spontaneity and adventure.

60

soccer tournament in Rochester Hills, Mich., we mused about getting tickets for that night's Detroit Red Wings-Chicago Blackhawks playoff game.

"There's tickets available but too bad," said Denny. "It's in Chicago."

I replied, *Then let's go to Chicago!*

He didn't hesitate. We set off in his Jeep, stopping only to buy Wings T-shirts (although I am a diehard Toronto Maple Leafs fan). We ordered the tickets online but, at the time, would have to pick up paper versions at the United Center box office. Fearing it would be closed by the time we arrived, I asked Denny to pull over at a Best Western.

I'll ask if we can use the printer in their business centre, I said.

"You're crazy. No one lets you use their business centre if you're not staying there."

Just leave it to me.

Five minutes later, having convinced the concierge that he would be my "hero of the day" if he bailed us out, I returned to the Jeep triumphantly waving two sheets of paper. Half-way through the five-hour drive, we looked at each other as if to say, "This was a pretty dumb idea, wasn't it?" But there was no turning back.

We missed the first period and the Wings lost, 4-1, which was fine with me, but we had the best time mocking the song piped over the public address speakers after Blackhawk goals, Chelsea Dagger by the Fratelli's. Denny said, "This is the most annoying goal song in the history of the NHL. It should be banned."

Immediately after the game we drove to Calumet, Indiana, so that in the morning, with an early start, we could make it for Calum's next game. We were in the stands for the opening whistle. Denny's parents, who were there, noticed the spark returning to him after the scarring of his divorce. They saw in me a kindred spirit who would share his passions.

I knew things were getting serious when Denny agreed to accompany me to a firefighter conference in Niagara Falls. It opened his eyes to the depth of MD's impact on my life. I was, at first, nervous that he might be frightened off, but just the opposite happened. He embraced their support and their culture. Unlike my first husband, he understood the importance of my networking with them. And, luckily for Denny, he knew how to party.

We had been dating for six months when the lease came up on the storage locker I rented after the divorce. I asked his advice on whether I should renew it and he was quick to suggest the more practical solution, that I move in with him. I got along well with his children and was usually there when it was their time to stay with him. They were unhappy if I returned to my parents' house. "You're not going anywhere. Move in and we'll see how it goes," Denny said. The decision wasn't a difficult one.

One night we were making dinner in his kitchen. I was sitting on the counter. He gave me a look that I will never forget. It was fiery and chill all at the same time, as if to say, You're OK. You're safe with me. I accept you, flaws and all. You're just Danielle and that's all I need. And in that moment, I knew: Being with Denny McLeod was like being in the water. I'm not disabled. No barriers. No limits. It was as if my life in the pool had come on land.

I consider myself a strong, independent woman, but in Denny I found my protector.

He is a typical techie: Do the facts support the decision? Does it make sense? What is the context? Is there a counter-argument? His moods are illuminated by the music he plays, and how loud he plays it. He is happiest on the musical fringes. Our wedding song was Biffy Clyro's Many of Horror. I dare you to name another bridal song with "horror" in the title. We were a "comfortable-in-our-own-skins" kind of couple. We chilled in jeans and T-shirts but cleaned up well if I was doing a speaking engagement.

On Christmas morning, we gathered around the tree in our pajamas with the kids. He insisted on me trying on my new sunglasses in the bathroom, so I could use the mirror. It struck me as odd, but I had become accustomed to Denny's carefully scripted special occasions. When I returned, Ella snatched up the final present under the tree, in a nondescript Amazon box, and asked her father whose name was on it. "It's for Danielle, honey." She handed me the box as Denny locked me in a stare. Inside the Amazon box, beneath a sheaf of pink wrapping paper, was zip-tied a small jewelry box. It goes without saying that what that box contained sent me into an ugly-cry, the kind that turns your makeup to goo.

"Will you marry me?"

More ugly-cry. Move on to puddle stage. So, THIS is what it is supposed to feel like.

Yes!

When the kids realized I was crying for joy and not sadness, Calum said, "Well, this means you will be with us forever." This prompted the mother of all ugly-cries. We would have a video of this scene had Denny turned on the camera he had planted in the tree. But with his window to give me the gift shrinking, he put down his phone without hitting the record button.

When we played it cool at family Christmas gatherings, holding off on formal announcements to see if anyone noticed the ring, the kids would blurt out that Daddy and Danielle were getting married. Ella wasted no time asking when we would have a baby.

We picked New Year's Eve at the Masonic Temple for our wedding reception so it would be as much a party as a formal celebration of our union. The non-denominational service was performed by a celebrant, Joe McParland, who was known for his entertaining and often humourous takes on the rites of marriage.

Our photos were taken at the historic Willistead Manor, which was decorated for Christmas, with the signature image taken on the grand staircase, with Ella and I at the top and Denny and Calum at the bottom. At the photographer's signal, I followed Ella down the steps, Denny followed Calum up, and we met in the middle with the kids front and centre. Our desire to make the wedding special for them was so strong that we dressed Ella's Elf on the Shelf figurine in a gown, got its hair done and brought it to the reception.

The party was off the charts and, after chastising us for making her staff carry an outrageous amount of alcohol into the hall, thinking it wasteful, the manager admitted that she had never seen so much consumed at a wedding. It was as if both families knew that after our disastrous first marriages, we were finally getting it right and they had even greater reason to celebrate.

Given my medical condition, we suspected we would need help to get pregnant. A nurse who is a friend of the family set us up with Dr. Rahi Victory, an obstetrician and fertility expert. He was self-confident to a fault, quick to pronounce, "I'm going to get you pregnant!" He was a doc you wanted in your corner. He was progressive in his thinking toward conception, using an eclectic array of home remedies to aid the cause. I was convinced that the drinking water in his clinic was part of his so-called "magic tricks."

The first months of our marriage were a joyful celebration of our mutual love of adventurous fun, clouded only by my monthly disappointment at the arrival of my menstrual period. It seemed all of my friends were getting pregnant, and I was attending baby showers on a weekly basis. I was taking the vitamins prescribed by Dr. Victory. I feared that after a sincere effort, Denny would check out, saying, "Well, we tried."

That old refrain from my childhood, "Why does it have to be so hard," reared its head amidst tearful breakdowns on my mother's shoulder. Our families rallied, with my parents offering to subsidize the more than $10,000 cost of invitro fertilization and my sister-in-law suggesting she would serve as a surrogate.

Denny's kids, Ella and Calum, were a centrepiece in our wedding.

In true Denny-Danielle style, we tackled our sadness with a road trip. We packed his Jeep for the 11-hour drive to Seaside Heights, on the Jersey Shore, where the British folk rock band Mumford & Sons was headlining the Gentlemen of the Road Stopover tour. For the first time since the area was ravaged by Hurricane Sandy, they were allowing camping on the beach.

We bought a loaf of bread and a jar of peanut butter to make sandwiches, reducing the number of stops. The hours we shared on Interstate 76 through the Pocono Mountains became a fist-pumping celebration of our wanderlust, fuelled by Denny's playlist blaring road-trip rock and a bottomless supply of Starbucks coffee.

At the nine-hour mark we stopped in Philadelphia so Denny could introduce me to his longtime friend Alison Dilworth, a freelance artist who was raised in Windsor and obtained her BA from the Tyler School of Art. On her website she describes herself as a freelance mural painter, book maker, writer, bone collector, typewriter junkie, amateur bird taxidermist, treasure hunter, teacher and birth doula. Her work involves building shrines to hold space for precious things that are difficult to articulate. Hanging with Alison kick-started the artsy vibe that would permeate the trip.

We caught a break when security mistakenly let us though a gate that allowed us to pitch our tent close to the Seaside Heights boardwalk, and park nearby, which was a bonus for Denny, who hauled most of our gear. We spent two nights in a two-person tent, waking to glorious sunrises over the Atlantic, with the boardwalk serving as a people-watching paradise and the pier acting as a dividing line between the concert venue and the campground. While the boardwalk was rich with a ski lift, amusement rides, games and carnival foods, the nearby streets and businesses were transformed into a bohemian's dream with artwork and pop-up stages.

The atmosphere was transcendent. Shark watchers were on the lookout for Mary Lee, a 50-year-old, 3,500-pound great white that had been tagged in 2012 and was reported cruising the Jersey Shore, sparking a certain Jaws vibe. We ate unusual coastal foods including a soft-shell crab sandwich that Denny insisted on, but I found disgusting. And so did he, but he ate it anyway. Everywhere around us were music nuts and campers, Denny's favourite people. I always considered myself outgoing, but Denny took it to the next level with our tent neighbours.

We shared stories and a potluck dinner, consuming large quantities of beer and rum. I enjoyed a contributor's buffalo chicken dip so much that it became my go-to potluck recipe. We played yard games on the beach, kept an eye out for Mary Lee and celebrated American Pharoah winning the Triple Crown two hours away at Belmont Park.

The Mumford concert was an adoring, two-hour sing-along in which most of the crowd knew the words to every song. When the set was over, we queued up like cattle to the beach exit ramp and wandered the boardwalk, people-watching. We partied into the wee hours then spent the night in an intimate celebration of our bond, on an air mattress fanned by a warm, fragrant ocean breeze, the sound of waves lightly lapping the shore. It was like making love on a cloud. A very sandy cloud.

Before leaving for home, we made a pact that we would drive until we couldn't stand the smell of each other, since we hadn't bathed for three days and reeked of sweat, sand and surf. Four hours from home, we pulled over, bought two of the largest bottles of Stella Artois beer we could find, got a hotel room, downed the beer in the shower and slept for 11 hours.

After the best of our many road trips, we returned home with great memories and an even greater surprise – I was pregnant.

I estimate that I was less than a minute late for my period when I awoke on the morning of Aug. 25 to a positive pregnancy test. I jumped on the bed and shook Denny awake, then raced off to the diner where my mother and Aunt Karen had their morning coffee. She knew by the smile on my face. She knew the significance of the date. Her mother had died on Aug. 25. I saw her eyes moisten.

My joy quickly gave way to apprehension. Can my body deliver on this pregnancy? Can I care for a newborn? What if I fall down? What if I drop him? Denny quelled my fears. I may not have been rock steady, but I was athlete tough when faced with a challenge. What's more, Denny had been through two births. When Corbin arrived following a routine pregnancy, Denny got back on the bike. He connected with that baby so naturally that my fears vanished.

To describe Denny as a cool customer would be an understatement. As if to prove it, and to bring a symmetrical conclusion to my pregnancy, at the five-month mark Denny took me to an All Them Witches concert at the Marble Bar, an indie club in a sketchy neighbourhood in Detroit. Why I agreed to attend a concert in such a precarious state, and with so much on the line, I can't say, but it speaks to the trust that my husband inspired in me.

Two years later Samson was conceived, unexpectedly. I took the pregnancy test at a friend's house across the street. Denny was summoned from grass cutting and my friend sat him down with a tall glass of whiskey. I was ecstatic. Denny, not so much. It was initially difficult for him, and in a deviation for us, we descended into radio silence on the baby front.

Following an uneventful pregnancy, Samson was born in respiratory distress and spent his first five days in the neonatal intensive care unit. It was our introduction to the pain and worry of caring for your children in hospital. My appreciation for parents who experience this is beyond estimation. The trauma of seeing his tiny body connected by tubes to that breathing machine, unable to cradle him, gave me the closest thing to PTSD that I can imagine.

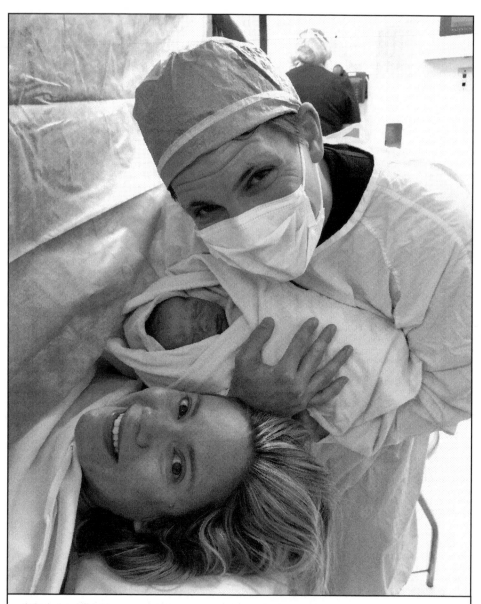

 Danielle Campo McLeod is with **Denny McLeod**.

April 25, 2021 · 🌐

5 years ago my heart was filled with the greatest joy. I'll never forget Dr. Victory Reproductive Care saying to us "your package has a package. Our beautiful little boy was born. Corbin has made us smile everyday since. To be blessed to know Corbin is to know adventure. He loves with his whole heart and his smile is pure joy. He is silly, fun, busy, loving, creative and so much more. Corbin mommy and daddy love you so much!!!! For 5 years we have smiled everyday because of you. Happy Birthday Corbin!!!!

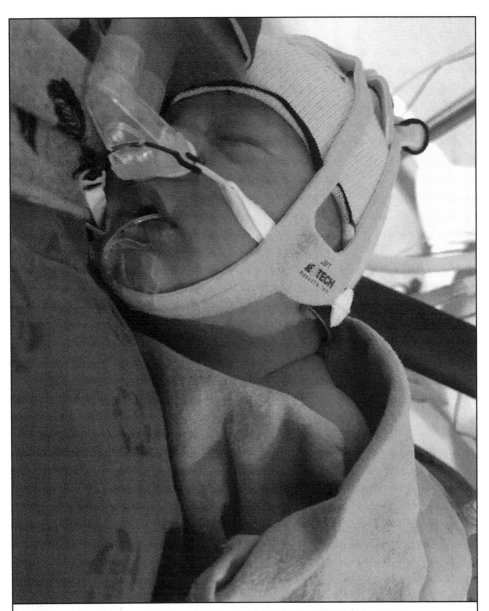

Danielle Campo McLeod is with **Denny McLeod** and **Steve Campo**.   ...
April 15, 2021 ·

My Dear Samson, you are perfect in every way. You came out and had a fight to win. But in true Sammy fashion you did it with strength and grace. You are my deep rooted connection to Pepe. You love life and love to smile. You are 100% a daddy's boy who loves to eat. I'm so blessed to be your mom. Happy 2nd birthday. I love being on every step of the journey of life with you. Thank you for choosing daddy and I to be your parents. Thank you for filling us with joy everyday! Happy 2nd Birthday

Easy on the Mayo

In the spring of 2020, sitting in my minivan with a life-altering diagnosis, I asked my specialist, how it is, Dr. Tarnopolsky, that I could go from muscular dystrophy to its treatable cousin? How do I not get angry about years of suffering that could have been avoided? How do I tell my parents? How do I tell the world?

Where do I go from here?

In adulthood I had begun to question whether I had MD. My body wasn't reacting the way doctors had forecast, as imprecise as those forecasts could be. I wanted to know if my kids were at risk.

With muscular dystrophy ruled out, my condition was identified as congenital myasthenic syndrome, or CMS. It is a rare autoimmune disorder caused by a gene mutation that is both readily detectable and relatively simple to treat. It is discovered in the genetic testing that did what muscle biopsies – how I was originally diagnosed – could not.

According to the National Organization for Rare Disorders, or NORD, in CMS an out-of-whack gene can disrupt the communication between motor nerves and muscle fibers. It is a highly specialized process involving the chemicals acetylcholine, sodium and calcium, and the molecules acetate and choline. This results in an abnormal protein or even loss of a protein that impairs some part of the process in which the nerves tell the muscles what to do.

"We don't actually think it's a muscular issue," Dr. Tarnopolsky told me in that June 2020 phone call. "It's more of a nerve issue. Which makes it like a neuron neuropathy." In other words, my nerves were talking Italian and my muscles French – just like the Campo family. The new drug regimen would act like a neuropathic Switzerland.

As crazy as it sounds, in 33 years I had never taken a prescription drug for muscular dystrophy. Braces, yes. Prayer, a whole lot. But not a single pill. There had been no miracle cures until, hopefully, now.

The new treatment would consist of Mestinon, a drug which stimulates chemicals in the body that affect communication between nerve impulses and muscle movement, and ephedrine, a jack-of-all-trades stimulant often prescribed for weight loss. Ephedrine's job would be to give the Mestinon a kick in the butt. The U.S. Food and Drug Administration approved Mestinon to treat soldiers exposed to nerve gas in the Gulf War. It's been around since the 1950s.

"I don't know how your response to the treatment is going to be but we're going to give it a try," said Dr. Tarnopolsky. "We'll send the Mestinon by mail and you can get the ephedrine in a health food store."

"It's going to give you better muscle response. It's going to call the nerves to wake them up, so they will get the messages a lot faster."

"OK?" he said. "We'll be in touch."

I didn't know what to think or how to react. Picking myself up off the floor of my van, I said, OK, and we hung up.

Now what? My parents had not seen this coming. I could only imagine their reaction after years of coping and hoping. Parents of children with disabilities are not prone to instant jubilation like in the movies. They develop a low-expectation mechanism so as not to be heartbroken.

Mine dealt with their daughter's condition in profoundly different ways. Mom and I were cut from the same cloth – everything is on the table. Dad was more of an internalizer. He is regulator of the "ordinariness" in my life. Telling him about the diagnosis reminded me of calling to report my world record at Christchurch. *Dad, I'm the best at something – on the ENTIRE PLANET!* So, to test the impact of this news, I decided to call him first.

I said to him, *Dad, I've got to tell you something. Remember when I broke my first world record? I called you and had to explain that I'm the fastest person in the whole world. Do you remember how you felt?*

He said, "Danielle, I'm cutting the grass. What are you talking about?"

He was irritated by having his chores interrupted, but I needed his absolute attention. No different than the world record. No different than the time they made me swim with eight-year-olds. I needed the type of validation only my father could give.

This is important Dad. My doctor in Hamilton has found the name of the genetic disorder that I have. It's called myasthenic syndrome.

"OK, so what?" Dad replied.

71

When I said, *He's sending me a treatment,* the line went silent. It was exactly the reaction of 22 years ago when I broke the world record. And I found in that silence the validation I needed — he had been rendered speechless by its significance.

I said, *I don't know exactly what this means but I will take this medication and we will see what happens.* And his response was, "Oh, all right. Gotta go."

I could tell my dad was crying.

Telling Mom was a different story. She was at my house with Denny, helping with the kids, and I ordered them all upstairs.

You guys have to sit down. Mark Tarnopolsky just called. My diagnosis has changed and there's a treatment. A prescription drug. I start when it arrives in the mail.

Mom was cautious. "Huh, interesting."

Denny looked excited, sort of, but also hesitant.

We had been chasing a genetic solution for a decade and they didn't share my instant high. "You have to remember," Mom said, "that 35 years ago our world was shattered."

I said, *You guys are mood killers! This is really exciting!*

Denny said, "I'll be excited when I see that you respond to the medication."

Mom started to warm to the idea of a miracle but was not yet ready for a happy dance. "Danielle, this is what Dad and I have been praying for for 35 years. I can't just flick a switch and be as excited as you, like this is a dream come true."

My in-laws were not conditioned to guard against false hope, and their reaction mirrored mine. Straight to unbridled excitement. Linda cried and Allan said, "This is amazing!" Then my mom walked into the room carrying a laundry basket, joking, "I guess I won't have to do this again." She was only beginning to process the notion that her daughter could live a long, normal life. I had no idea the emotional Pandora's box that I had unlocked for my parents.

And with that, we returned to our regularly scheduled programming. No tears of joy. No champagne. No Facebook updates. Just a nascent flicker of hope.

Denny slipped into researcher mode, learning through the internet that Mestinon achieved significant gains for people in my condition. He explained it to me in layman's terms. "Danielle, it's going to wake up the nerves. With the ephedrine, instead of saying "Wake up" in a whisper, it's going to yell. "WAKE UP!"

The medication arrived and I didn't know whether to set off fireworks or curl up in the fetal position. What if it doesn't work? What if the results are in my imagination? This could crush my soul and take my parents back to a dark place. I was nervous.

Denny is a techie and I'm an elite athlete, so the answer was a simple one – conduct a trial. Measure the results. We hatched a plan for me to do squats before and after taking the first pill. We would record them on video. And if I felt the least bit better, it would be worth it. Expectations managed.

But when it came to executing the strategy, my fear of disappointing everyone took hold. I was alone in my kitchen when I swallowed the first pink pill with an ephedrine chaser. And then I proceeded to make the kids' sandwiches.

The mayonnaise jar would be the first test of my miracle pill, and I would be the only one to see the result: can I rip off the protective tab with my hands instead of my teeth, as I usually do? I felt a tingling in my finger, like your foot just before it falls asleep. Then I felt it all over. The left side of my face. The right. Oh God, I thought, *I'm having a stroke!* Is it the ephedrine? I felt energized, like I could make sandwiches for an army.

I grabbed the mayonnaise, said a prayer and, voila, the tab was in my grasp. I froze in disbelief. By this time Denny was behind me and he said, "What. Just. Happened?" Not yet ready to accept the outcome, I joked, *Yeah, the lid must have been loose. Just a coincidence.* I did not want to tell anyone I took the meds and opened a mayo jar as easily as flipping a coin.

As an athlete I am in tune with my body. I can detect the slightest change in how my muscles fire. After the mayo conquest, something was different. Weird. I felt like I was firing ... faster. I did not know if it was the ephedrine, the Mestinon, or a figment of my imagination, but I was not going to stop there. I walked up a flight of stairs and my muscles felt less fatigued. It was like a fog in my brain that I never realized was there had burned off.

And when my family heard the news, their reaction was predictably light: "Dear God, strap on your seatbelts," Mom said, "because Danielle is on ephedrine."

I felt better from the start but on the third day of Mesti-phedrine, the pain relief went to a new level. I went to bed after a day of strenuous activity with the kids and my feet did not hurt. All my life I thought everyone went to bed with aching feet because of the wear on their Achilles tendons. No, but you do when you have untreated CMS.

Body part by body part, I ticked off a list of things that feel better. My leg pain was gone. My back pain was gone. I was sleeping better, an unexpected bonus since insomnia is a side-effect of ephedrine. I was waking up in the morning and not needing a forklift to get out of bed. I could go about my business the minute my feet hit the floor. And I would have been happy with that.

But it got better. Way better. I was able to help with the kids without fatiguing so quicky. Corbin asked, "Mommy can you play dinosaurs with me?" We would normally do this on the couch to make it easier for me, but I told him, let's play on the floor. Yet another test. Not only could I get eye level with my five-year-old, but I stood up without having to strain my arms.

"What the heck?" said Denny, now fully bought into test driving the new me. "You need to do the stairs without hanging on to the railing." I scaled them easily – more stable and not watching every step with dread. No rails. No falls. I couldn't wait to tell Dr. Tarnopolsky.

Holy crap, I said. *It's Day 4 and all these amazing things have happened. My nerves are calling my muscles, and my muscles are answering.*

"We've got to get you to Hamilton," the doctor said. "We have to get some actual strength tests on you and see what's going on."

By Canada Day we were celebrating my ability to squat, climb stairs, attend to the kids and more. I began bathing them at night when I would normally be whacked out lifting them in and out of the tub.

You can only imagine the effect of this on my relationship with Denny. It changed from one of dependency to an equal partnership in the care of our kids. He didn't have to be four steps ahead of everything because now I was physically able to walk them to the park, play on the equipment, climb the ladders and fly down a slide. I excelled at the children's tag game What Time is it Mr. Wolf?

Even my swimming stroke changed because now I could fully engage my legs. The sensations I felt in my competitive days started to return, only better. Friends joked that I was risking having my medals taken away. "Does this mean you were cheating?"

No, it isn't cheating when you find out 20 years after your Paralympic days that you were misdiagnosed. The Paralympics only care about the state you were in when you competed, and I was a bona fide S7.

The effect on my parents was profound. For the first time they could exhale. Their daughter would not have to worry about what the future holds or how she would take care of herself.

Word got out and I was besieged by interview requests. My swimming career had made me a hometown celebrity and now I was back in the spotlight. Everyone likes a fairytale ending, right? Two weeks into my new life and embarrassed that I had not told close friends and family, I posted a Facebook video explaining what had happened.

I am living my best life, I said, *and I challenge you to do the same.*

By this time, I was employed by Muscular Dystrophy Canada as director of quality assurance and program development. And even though I did not technically have MD, I was proof that genetic testing, which was ever-evolving,

Danielle Campo McLeod
July 20, 2020 · 🌐   •••

Just a mom holding her baby. No pain!!!!!!

could offer hope for a treatment. The news invigorated MDC.

Even my supervisor noticed the improvement. I was not so fatigued that I had to be excused from 4:30 meetings. "I'm not afraid that I burnt you out completely," she said. "You're flying out projects better. I see that you are sharper on things. We need to get you out on the road." But plans for a speaking tour were derailed by the COVID pandemic.

Dr. Tarnopolsky was delighted that aside from producing more saliva, I did not suffer side-effects. I wish now that I had documented the saliva issue because it would come into play in the health crisis that, unknown to me, was looming.

"One more thing," Dr. Tarnopolsky said. "You need to be done having kids." The ephedrine in my drug cocktail would prevent me from getting pregnant.

Denny and I looked at each other and laughed. He had two children from a previous marriage. We've had two together, both by C-section.

No worries, doc, our family is complete. We're happy and the drugs are working to perfection. We have a new path, free of pain. I'm going to focus on my career.

We entwined our hands, stared into Dr. T's eyes and exclaimed, "We. Are. So. Done!"

I am often asked, why did it take 33 years for a correct diagnosis. "Are you angry, Danielle?" And my reply is no, you can't be angry. I understand that science is ever-evolving and I'm excited that it did this for me. My family and I have long advocated for clinical trials and funding for research. We enjoyed the support of firefighters who backed us with their boot campaigns. We viewed my new diagnosis as the outcome. Today, doctors can test millions of DNA strands, raising the odds for more people with muscular dystrophy to get a second chance. My doctor tested 32,000 strands before identifying my condition.

Still, when at times I found myself questioning why it took so long, I found comfort in the words of a woman I met as news spread globally of my changed fate. The woman was not prescribed Mestinon until her 70s. Her 70s! "You don't get to be angry Danielle. You're 35 years old. You have your whole life ahead of you. What happened has shaped the person you are today."

The hardest thing to deal with was the perception of me. Only after regaining my strength did I realize the depth of limitation that people associated with me. And with my limits changing, a new understating of how people viewed the pre-Mestinon me.

As the expectations increased, so did my grasp of how I had been coddled. I never thought people treated me differently. But suddenly I was being involved in everything. I was in on the joking. I felt more included without having to try to be included or make it work. It upset me that I didn't realize how different my life was with a disability label.

For God's sake, I told audiences at guest speaking events, *give people their own voice. Don't assume you know what they need.* Mom knew what I meant. I needed help carrying laundry baskets up the stairs because I might fall. I didn't need it to clean the floor. One she would do, the other she wouldn't touch.

I realized how much of the load Denny carried in our household. It angered me that I was blind to the accommodations. Only when they were gone did I realize they were there in the first place.

It's the psychological war I waged within myself.

Another Big Load of Potatoes

On the way home from Dr. Tarnopolsky's office in Hamilton, we laughed about the specialist telling us no more kids. "We're so DONE!" Things had finally come together and we were not about to unwind them.

I took this drug combo for a few months. I was concerned about the long-term effects of ephedrine, which had been linked to heart conditions. After consulting with Dr. T. we made the decision to see what Mestinon could do on its own without the boost from ephedrine.

For two weeks Mestinon seemed to be holding its own. Then I started experiencing nausea, fatigue and brain fog. I wanted to start taking the ephedrine but didn't. My family doctor ordered a blood test and the result was confirmed by Dr. Victory.

I was pregnant.

And panicked.

You're joking, right? I told the OB. *It's this office. Everybody pees positive in your office, right? You're a fertility specialist for crying out loud.*

But there was no getting around it and no sense beating around the bush with Denny. *Surprise! It wasn't the medication making me so tired! Number 5 is on its way!* I sat him down with a tumbler of whiskey. And he knew instantly why because that is how I primed him for the surprise announcement of Samson.

"You've got to be kidding me," he exclaimed. We laughed, hugged and he said, "Well, here we go again!"

Except, it was not so simple. The laughter faded and a dreadful realization set in. I would have to halt the drugs that had changed my life. There was no question I would stop taking ephedrine, which is proven to be harmful during

My mom, Colleen, is my rock. This is our favourite photo.

pregnancy. There was also no evidence to suggest that Mestinon was safe for my unborn child. No research said it would be OK for a pregnant woman with a neuromuscular disorder.

I had always been a careful mom-to-be, swearing off wine, chocolate and even sushi – which can carry high levels of mercury – while I carried the two boys. The thought of my daughter being born with health issues because of medication I was taking was too much to bear. I would stop the meds and do what I always do – tough it out.

What for me was a no-brainer was a struggle for Denny and my dad. They feared for me. Dad was angry that we allowed this to happen, and not afraid to say so. "You're in such a great place, physically," he said. Which upset me. *Dad, you do not get to decide this. It's our family. WE decide this.*

As for Mom, she was put on this earth to be a grandmother. She said: "All your life you have done everything that people told you to do, or not to do. Nobody can tell you not to have a baby. It is just God's plan for you. I can't not be happy."

Denny was in a perpetual state of worry, struggling to summon the excitement of an expectant dad. As my pain and weakness returned, he was saddened to see that I once again needed help with the kids and the household. I started to wonder if my body could withstand another pregnancy with two little ones needing attention. And I did not have Mestinon, my Popeye spinach, to save the day.

The kids were confused. Mommy was doing all these things, and now she's tired again. What's going on?

There was, of course, a second option. The nuclear option: Terminate the pregnancy. While I entertained the discussion, reluctantly, with Denny, in reality there was zero chance I would agree. I was raised in a devout Roman Catholic family with an Italian-Canadian dad and a French-Canadian mom. Abortion? Not for me. Denny, who was raised in the United Church, was living in dread that the pregnancy would harm his wife. He took up the other side of the debate.

It was a crisis moment in our marriage. Conceiving a child was our mistake. And in my view, it was our responsibility to carry it through. We thought we couldn't get pregnant but it happened. *This baby has been sent to us,* I thought. *She is coming. Who are we to play God?* My life has been a series of challenges which were placed at my feet for a reason. So if this baby was not supposed to be here, I would not be pregnant.

And, selfishly, I will admit that I wanted the baby to be a girl. I wanted that instant replay of my mom's jubilation when she announced she was pregnant with me.

"But you are in such a good place right now, so healthy," Denny said. "I'm just scared." On our third date he promised to have one child with me. Not two. Certainly not three. His context was different than mine.

After a few days of tense back-and-forth, we were back into the radio silence that preceded Samson's birth. Hard to do in a household with four kids, but we managed. Meals were taken in silence. We holed up in separate rooms. Even our goodnight kisses were perfunctory. I didn't try to poison him with supercharged chicken wings, but the thought crossed my mind.

We had exhausted our capacity to discuss it. For the time being, I would carry the excitement of this pregnancy on my own.

With Denny, Samson, Calum and the inverted Corbin, awaiting the new arrival

During that downtime I took stock. Yes, we could focus on the negatives: everything from my health to our little bungalow being too small for a fifth child. Or we could focus on the positives: I am the healthiest that I have been in ages and all signs point to the fetus being fine.

I stopped the medication. Cold turkey. I could not bring myself to swallow another pill knowing it might harm this baby.

It remained a touchy subject for us – with Mom in my corner and Dad in Denny's. I wondered if, in the wake of my divorce, ending a pregnancy would be a bridge too far for my religious mother.

When the first ultrasound showed a strong, healthy heartbeat, Denny's fears started to diminish. She was perfect. This was happening. I told Denny that if something goes wrong in this pregnancy and the baby is not born, at least I can say I was a mom to a daughter for a little while.

Placenta previa is the medical term for the placenta shifting until it covers the opening of the uterus. It often happens with women who have had C-sections and can cause complications including bleeding. At about the 12-week mark, I got it bad with this little one and following an ultrasound, Dr. Victory prescribed no heavy lifting. This threw Denny back a bit, rekindling his fear that I would either suffer a medical decline or lose the baby. The what-ifs from early in the pregnancy came flooding back. I tried to lead by example, dealing with the stress by reaffirming my belief that the outcome was in God's hands.

At about the 30-week mark the placenta moved out of the way. Crisis averted. Which isn't to say I was not in pain and chronically fatigued. I was; I chose not to tell anyone. My legs. My back. It was like they were being pierced by daggers. My hands were so weak that I reverted to opening the mayo jar with my teeth.

With COVID lockdowns, I was working from home but not letting on to my employer than I was suffering. I didn't want to make it real. Naming it makes it real. I tried to convince myself that Denny didn't know but we were sharing an office in our home. Of course he knew. He was 100 per cent on it. He read the telltale signs, noting how my sleep was disturbed. My pain and weakness got worse than before I started on Mestinon. It was the third time I put a challenged body through this, and it was pushing back. I gained 45 pounds compared to 30 from my previous pregnancies.

Finally, in my mind, the switch went off. I was tired of being pregnant and ready for it to be over. I was done. The final nine weeks would be all about hanging on.

For years I have shared my life story on Facebook. On May 27, I posted my gratitude to be expecting a perfectly healthy baby girl. Privately, I was counting down the days until I could resume taking Mestinon.

> **Danielle Campo McLeod** •••
> May 27, 2021 · 🌐
>
> So Grateful to be expecting a healthy baby girl. I feel blessed that this body allowed me to have children. The last few days I have woken up with more muscle pain and weakness everyday. I have not been taking my medication since finding out I was pregnant. Yesterday a quick trip to the OB triage just to make sure leg pain wasn't anything serious. Today as I have to transition back into the old way I use to due things before my medication. I can't help but be thankful. Thankful because I will have another baby that will complete our family. But also thankful because I have a treatment that allows me to live strong and pain free. So today I will give this a pain a purpose. I will offer to all those that live everyday in pain. To everyone that doesn't have a treatment. To all those parents that will hear their child has a disability and all those adults that will have lived life one way and have to change because of a new diagnosis. If you need to be lifted up today I offer this pain to you. #attitude

To make matters worse, my activity was restricted by COVID. The pools were closed, so I could not swim out the pain like before. There was no massage therapy. All my tactics (I call them vices) to get me through the day were gone. I hid in my office because I didn't want the kids to know I was working from home because I wouldn't have had a moment's peace. I was singularly focused on the sequence of events when the newborn arrives: See baby. Hold baby. Take pills.

I researched like nobody's business and there was no evidence that breastfeeding on Mestinon would be a problem. The chances of it transferring to my breast milk were remote, doctors told me. My attitude was, *Baby, you are going to learn how to digest this. This is happening.*

I repeated to myself, *Find your anchor* – the mental push to stay on the right side of the dark cloud that preys on us when we are in pain.

Every day, and sometimes moment by moment, I paused to reflect on what gave me joy: the pleasure of having my children at the dinner table, the warm rush of them piling on to our bed in the morning, making PBJs at lunch. Denny.

***

Pepe exercised religiously and didn't smoke, so in January 2020 when my mother told me he had terminal lung cancer, I couldn't believe it. I was in my car when she called to say the doctors found a mass. I pounded the steering wheel and screamed, *No! No! No! Not him!* When Pepe had tried to talk to me about his eventual death, I refused to listen.

I set up a temporary office in his apartment kitchen so I could be near him while I worked. He exercised until his body wouldn't tolerate it anymore, using an overhead bar to pull himself out of bed rather than ask for help. Still, a family member was always there to keep watch. We enjoyed some of our best heart-to-hearts in those final months.

His health declined rapidly. Watching him deteriorate from a strong, independent man to being incapacitated broke my heart. That Father's Day, my brothers and I posed for photographs with our grandfather, knowing they would probably be the last. He soldiered on without complaint – we shared that trait – but one day while seated next to me in his rocking chair, he broke down in tears. "Don't worry, Kiddo," he said. "I'm not going anywhere, because even if I'm not here, I'm here."

I said, *Not you, Pep. Anyone but you.*

He replied, "It's just my turn."

The last thing I said to him was, *I love you. I will keep counting the hawks.*

A week before my scheduled Cesarean section, Aug. 12, 2021, Mom suggested a visit to Pepe's gravesite. We staged a selfie/silhouette photo in which Mom's hand reached out to my tummy, superimposed over his headstone. It symbolized the bond we shared and how he continued to inspire me. He was my hero, the carrier of my pain, scars and battles. In spirit, I had brought every struggle and fear of this pregnancy to him. My body breaking down again. The return of the muscle weakness. The week-by-week countdowns and praying on my knees for this little girl to be OK. I needed an infusion of Pepe's spirit.

As we knelt in prayer at his headstone, where we laid him to rest one year earlier, I felt at peace.

It was as if I could hear Pepe say, "It's just another big load of potatoes."

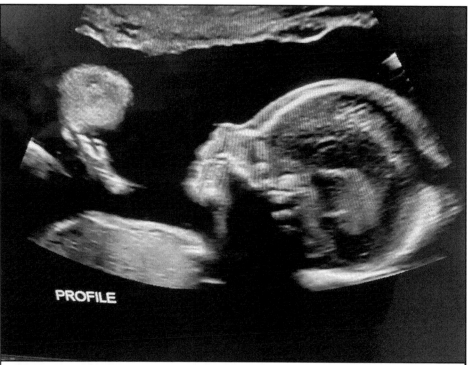

PROFILE

 Danielle Campo McLeod is with **Denny McLeod**.
January 30, 2021 · 🌐

Denny and I wanted to keep up our good news train of 2020 rolling into 2021. How do we top our great news of 2020. How about this? We are thrilled to announce our family is growing by one more. The van seats are now full. Baby McLeod will arrive at the end of August. I'm feeling incredible! Typical pregnancy symptoms but strong and healthy. I couldn't feel more blessed to get to experience a pregnancy in this new healthy body. The whole family can't wait to meet the final member of team McLeod!

You Can't Go Home

After weeks of indecision, we picked Morgan as the name of our child-to-be. In the waiting room of an OB triage clinic, where I was being examined for cramping, a voice on the public address system said, "Paging Dr. Danielle Morgan." Hospital pages never include a first name, so we took this as an omen. Morgan it is.

She was supposed to be delivered by Dr. Victory at 8 a.m. on Aug.18, 2021, at the Metropolitan Campus of Windsor Regional Hospital. And I was supposed to be home three days later.

I chose 8 a.m. because that was when Corbin was born and it went off without a hitch. You wake up, fast for a while and the moment is now. A series of ultrasounds showed a healthy fetus. Morgan was ready for prime time. I was ready to be that Pinterest mom with a complete set of offspring. I had fought through the withdrawal from Mestinon and was as physically ready as I could be. Training for the Paralympics taught me coping skills. I knew how to power through pain and program my mind for challenges.

Two days before my scheduled date, I couldn't cope anymore. Suffering from excruciating back pain which I suspected was contractions, I contacted my OB about moving up the delivery.

At 11:10 p.m. we headed for the hospital. I had a moment of doubt in the car ride, thinking that maybe my pain wasn't so bad that I didn't need to rush things. That moment passed. I regretted that I couldn't say goodbye to the boys in the way I had planned, with them blowing bubbles as a distraction.

Once I was admitted to the hospital, I was uncomfortable and miserable enough to make Roseanne Barr look like a motivational speaker. And I was starting to get a bad feeling about the impending birth.

Things looked up when they applied the epidural. The needle hit its target on the first try. Hooray to the anesthesiologist! Likely due to my scoliosis, Corbin had taken three attempts and Samson five.

I thought I was home free, but I wasn't. The epidural wasn't working its magic. On the delivery table I told the doctor that I was in pain. This was my third C-section, so I knew the drill. Something was different. Something was wrong. But according to the medical team, I was completely numb. It was charting to be a textbook delivery.

Denny saw it too. He had been on heightened alert since we found out I was pregnant. We suppressed it at the time, but now we shared a sense of dread. Something bad was coming. I didn't know if it was fear because I've already had two C-sections or the knowledge that the six-week recovery from this one would be torture. I was not jubilant about the impending arrival of my daughter.

I prayed that nothing happened to me so I could get home to my boys. The baby needed to be OK. I worried she would spend time in the neonatal intensive care unit, like Samson did. Everyone assured me that my vital signs were good and we were on track. But the pain in my abdomen was like nothing I had ever experienced. They gave me extra oxygen to calm me down.

At 7:12 a.m. on Aug. 17, Morgan Colleen Linda McLeod was born, six pounds, two ounces, all pink and plump and the picture of health.

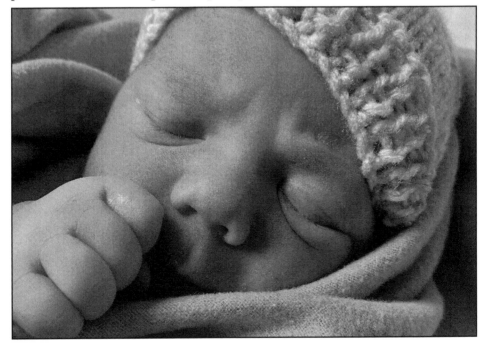

In the recovery room, I grappled with whether something had gone wrong in delivery or was it all in my head. Morgan was perfectly healthy, thank God. Me, not so much. I felt like I had just been beaten up. It was not the joyous arrival I had hoped for. My previous C-sections left scar tissue in my abdomen. I wondered if it complicated the delivery.

In the recovery room, my pain was matched by anguish. An athlete scans her body, going over a checklist of parts to make sure they're working. How is my leg strength today? My lung capacity? As I lay in the hospital bed, I patted my gut to see if I was bleeding. I wasn't.

Denny was gone. He left to check on Morgan. I felt alone as I retreated deeper into my reverie.

I was not the same mom as I was when Corbin and Samson were born. Instead of asking to nurse Morgan, I begged for pain meds. I didn't admit to Denny the severity. I reverted to the expert faker. After all, this was the pregnancy everyone questioned.

All my life it had been muscular dystrophy stealing the joy. Now it was a completely new malfunction getting in the way. What happened to my picture-perfect moment, the one in which I fling open a window and shout to the hilltops my elation at giving birth to a daughter?

Here she is! Here is my daughter! She is perfect! And I am fine! I will be a normal mom and we will be a normal family!

When I saw Morgan for the first time, Denny snapped a photo. I'm smiling but there was a look on my face that only Denny would recognize. It was "gritted-teeth pissed-off Danielle." To this day Denny struggles with that photo because he sees through my disguise.

Left, the moment I first saw Morgan. Right, an indifferent looking mom showing signs of postpartum depression.

As relieved as I was that Morgan was healthy, I was disappointed with my reaction. *This is your first time seeing her,* I thought. *Let your body do whatever it's going to do and focus on her. Just smile. It's going to be OK. Just smile.* That's the conversation I had with myself, that I must prove to everyone that this pregnancy was not a terrible idea. I was right to make this choice.

Why did I need this to be perfect? Why was it not OK that it was not OK? I am still trying to figure that one out, but what I know for certain is that the new diagnosis of my neuromuscular disorder, and with it the meds that took away a lifetime of pain, had changed my outlook on life. I had taken on a new identity as *Normal Mom* and I did not want to go back.

I wanted a woot-woot moment where Daddy cradles his baby and her siblings smother her with kisses. All pink balloons and marching bands.

I did not want to be wracked with guilt about the story I would tell my daughter, how this pregnancy was shrouded in second-guessing. This was not going to be about ill-fitting prom dresses and dangerous shoes. As soon as I am out of here, I thought, my Popeye spinach will kick in and I will jump rope instead of swinging it. I would no longer ask the question of my lifetime, *Why does this have to be so hard?*

And for the first time I wondered, was I selfish in having this child? Did I ask too much of a body that had been taxed since age two? Was I obsessed with retracing my mother's steps – the joy she experienced in learning she was having a daughter. To have my own little girl to cuddle and nurture and mentor; to have *that* talk about boys and debate what age is proper for her own cellphone?

Had I put everything we had achieved, every mountain we had climbed, at risk?

It was a helluva way to spend the first week with my newborn.

The meds they gave me were strong but the pain was stronger. As if preparing for battle, angry emotions churned inside me like tank sprockets. They set off an alarm so great, it pissed me off.

I desperately wanted the doctors to tell me what they said three days after Samson was born: "You can go home now. There is no reason to keep you." Days passed and the subject of my discharge never came up. The abdominal pain was not going away.

My mother noticed that I was not as connected to Morgan as I was to the boys. She worried postpartum depression was setting in. If there is such a thing as going through the motions when a newborn is suckling your breast, I was doing it.

My bowels were not working, which is not unusual after giving birth but was starting to drag on. Days passed without my bowels awakening and I could not go home until they did. This was unacceptable. You're supposed to deliver your baby, eat whatever you want, poop your brains out and head home to an adoring family. Pink balloons and a marching band. You are not supposed to keep your boys waiting.

By Day 3 the bloating in my abdomen was getting worse. The nurses listened for bowel sounds that never came. Each time they heard nothing, I felt like I failed a test. They concluded the delivery caused ileus, in which your colon stops making the wave-like movements that push broken-down food and waste to your butt so you can poop. This so-called "stunning" of the bowel is not uncommon, but in my state of mind I was a failure.

Hour by hour my condition declined. The pain was so intense that I don't remember the boys visiting. I hardly interacted with Morgan. I was too weak to feed her, so the nurses supplemented with formula. Denny thought, "Something is missing: Your motherly instinct. You're not even holding her."

Denny set up camp next to my hospital bed with an air mattress to sleep on, changes of clothes, some snacks and his ear buds. He brought a sterilizer for Morgan's formula bottles. It was becoming a long haul.

Two of my OB nurses, Olivia and Caitlin, were angels of mercy. Young, beautiful and brimming with optimism, not yet exhausted by the demands of their profession and genuine in their caring, they allowed themselves to become personally invested in Denny and me. Olivia once confided in me that she broke up with a boyfriend because their relationship didn't measure up to what Denny and I had. Caitlin shared her experiences renovating a home and was prone to say, "What the heck?" when things in my case didn't add up.

One day in the bathroom my pain reached a crescendo and I pulled the emergency cord. Olivia said, enough is enough, and a decision was made to insert a nasogastric tube, which typically carries food and medicine to the stomach through the nose. In my case it was used to vacuum the contents of my stomach so the bowel could rest.

You haven't lived until you go through the insertion of an NG tube, but at this stage, I was game for anything. Denny described it as a scene from the Exorcist. When the tube went in, three scud missiles of projectile vomit, purple, black and putrid, each more disgusting than the other, came out. I was nothing if not an equal opportunity spewer. I covered everyone in the room.

"Oh my Lord," said Olivia. "You put your insides on your outside." When, later, the tube had to be shoved in another six centimetres, to 56 total, I said to Olivia, *Are we talking about a man's six centimetres, or a real six centimetres?* Olivia laughed so hard she had to momentarily stop the procedure.

"I'm going to go and get your insides off of me," Olivia said.

Something about my husband covered in the rainbow-coloured remains of my last meal caused my emotions to boil. What I'm putting this man through is too much to ask, I thought. I wanted the world to know what he meant to me, so I did what I often do: post to Facebook.

We are good during the good times but man we are incredible in the shit times. I have loved my husband with all my heart. But now I respect him with every part of me. He has held me and allowed me to cry just the way I need to and then kick my butt back in gear.

The tube wasn't helping. My decline accelerated. My doctors ordered X-rays that were inconclusive and a decision was made to do exploratory surgery in my abdomen – the second major procedure in that area in 10 days. It would be risky and my family was put on high alert.

Surgeons were surprised to find a life-threatening disaster zone in my gut. A piece of the colon was poking through the lining of my abdomen and a section had necrotized. Imagine getting a car door slammed on your hand. The organ was strangled. Dead.

The surgeon removed and resectioned a seven-inch chunk. A hernia that had formed between the sub-layer of muscle and bowel was repaired.

My mother posted: "I almost lost her. Hours away from a very different outcome."

Denny at Morgan's side.

91

Call An Ambulance

Never was a fart so eagerly anticipated. The bowel resection should have cleared the decks for my recovery and the first sign of progress would be my passing gas. I had been corresponding with Adam Purdy, an old Paralympic training partner, throughout the ordeal and he hit me with a bizarre request. "When you finally pass gas," he said, "I want you to record it and send it to me." Who asks someone to record a fart? Adam would. I couldn't say no. Each day he texted me for an update. "Did it happen? Did it happen?"

By some miracle we managed to record me passing gas, and it became the fart heard around the world. We shared it not only with Adam, but the entire family because, hey, that's what you do after a horrible ordeal. For the first time in what seemed like years, Denny and I burst out laughing. "Finally," he said, "a light situation. Things are starting to look up. Something's finally going in the right direction."

A day later I was well enough to post to Facebook, *Just keep fighting; there's no other choice.* A day after that came the welcome news that the NG tube was coming out. Because of COVID restrictions, I had limited access to my family. But the hospital granted exceptions to allow my dad to visit, then the boys. They prepped the then five-year-old Corbin to see his mom in tubes.

I had been in the hospital, away from my boys and disengaged from my newborn daughter, for 12 days. My mental health was frail. My attempts to snuggle with Morgan were laughably pathetic. The social worker in me said I was in the throes of postpartum depression. Among its many related conditions is anhedonia, a loss of interest in things that would normally bring pleasure, including the baby. The restlessness and edginess showed when my mom insisted that "walking would fix everything." Which only succeeded in pissing me off. *This isn't going to be fixed by strolling the hospital corridors, Mom.* The walker they supplied me collected dust.

I have almost no memory of the first month of my daughter's life. What I know of those harrowing weeks has been related to me by Denny and my mother. My Facebook posts provide insights into my troubled state of mind.

Danielle Campo McLeod
August 31, 2021 · 🌐

I'm too sad to answer questions right now. I just need prayers. But I will never again question if you were worth it. I'll fight as hard as I need to Morgan it may take longer than I thought but team McLEod Denny McLeod will be all together soon.

Mom sensed that I was not making progress; that I wasn't the ambitious, hard-driving and competitive Danielle who stood atop Paralympic podiums when her legs could hardly support her. She recalled watching me pass out from the pain.

She leaned heavily into her faith, urging prayers from her social media following and proclaiming, "I am sure the heavens are shouting her name as the amount of prayers has been astounding."

On Day 20 I told my mother, *I just want to go home. Are you sure I'm going to get better?*

Denny thought, or at least had convinced himself to think, that I was improving. He noted that I was sitting up more, but it also appeared to him that I had reached a plateau. I didn't want to miss Corbin's first day of school. We started asking about a discharge date.

In the days leading up to my release, according to my medical records,

Danielle Campo McLeod
September 7, 2021 · 🌐

The words will not justify in this post how I am feeling. I'm not yet the person I will be because of this 21 day fight for my life. I will do my work on all levels and get back to a place that serves me and most importantly my family, friends and ever person my path may cross. The word faith has a new meaning to me. Today I take a step forward in my truths and great fullness. Because it's the only strength I have. A hug from my husband pulled me out of a dark place many times. He carried my soul for me and though I'm not ready to take it back it yet the look in his eyes tells me it's safe and waiting. My three babies have a piece of me in them. I will pull myself back together seeing it in them and remembered. I will never be able to thank everyone for oxygen. You see, every single time I read your message, it's like you were holding. You all kept me alive. I will be honest with you ever step of the way with how I am doing. I don't my own thoughts right now and im fighting to get them back. I will! Right now I own my breath and I will continue to breathe in time I will thank everyone. This will be my most difficult first day of school. What I do know is we were all in this together and we did it.
I'M COMING HOME TODAY

doctors noted steady improvement. The answer to our question about discharge came. It would be Sept. 7, the Tuesday after Labour Day. One day before the resumption of classes.

Denny thought that I was healthy enough to come home. Not perfect, but the remainder of the recovery would happen in a warm and familiar environment. His excitement was tempered by the fact that I had been in the hospital for 21 days.

The house was loud and full of family when I got home. Mom shot a video of the great reveal – that moment where the boys were allowed into the living room to greet me. Corbin plowed into my lap while Samson was more interested in his baby sister. I was emotional but oddly reserved.

The next morning came the second red flag as Denny pushed me in a wheelchair to Corbin's school. Every bump in the sidewalk sent bolts of pain to my abdomen. *Ouch. Ouch. Why are you hitting all the bumps Denny?*

"Why is it so painful Danielle? I didn't expect this. I knew it would take some time, but..."

The recoveries from my previous C-sections had not gone this way, but then again, they hadn't been accompanied by a bowel resection. It made sense. Sort of.

Mom was paying close attention to my mental state given how disconnected from the kids I had been in the hospital. Her professional training told her it could take months to recover. She was heartened when I expressed interest in breast-feeding Morgan.

When she summoned a relative who specialized in lactation to serve as my coach, the nurse was struck by my poor state of health.

At 6 p.m. on Sept. 8 I called Denny to my bedside and to his great shock, asked him to call an ambulance. Something was wrong. I couldn't breathe. My abdomen was bloated. My skin was the color of a tombstone. The paramedics realized that my heart was failing – the medical term is cardiomyopathy – and they rushed me to the emergency room of the very hospital I left a day earlier. Denny packed a hospital bag and jumped into his Jeep to meet us there, not yet aware of how critically ill I was. Ever the optimist, he was hoping a modest hospital procedure would get me home.

By 8 p.m. we were in the emergency room and it was discovered that my abdomen was wracked with infection. My white blood cell count was off the charts, five times normal and a sign of life-threatening toxins. I was vomiting and my color was ghostlike. A peripherally inserted central catheter, or PICC line, was inserted to administer antibiotics. Surgery was scheduled for first thing in the morning. I was wheeled to the intensive care unit.

In the ICU waiting room, Denny saw something that he took as a good omen. On the magazine rack was a copy of a local magazine that was dedicated to my change of diagnosis in 2020. He opened it to the article and a ripped-out page, which had served as a bookmark, fell to the floor. He took it as a positive sign and went home for a catnap feeling hopeful.

My mother was at our house, changing Morgan's diaper, when her phone rang. My name appeared on the screen. She was shaken. I wanted to talk to her before I went into surgery. I suspect that I feared I would not survive. In a slurred and barely audible voice I said, *Mom, I'm going to be OK.*

"I know honey. You're going to be OK."

So, you know how I want my kids raised, I said. *So, you be there, OK?* While I knew Denny would be a great dad, I was telling my mom that I wanted my kids to know how dearly she held her faith.

It dawned on my mother that I had called to say goodbye. Perhaps, a final goodbye. Not only was she losing her only daughter but the kids were losing their mom. Denny would find someone else. She had lived in a stepfamily when Pepe remarried six months after Tllly died. She didn't want that for Corbin, Samson and Morgan. She certainly didn't want it for herself.

What do you tell your only daughter in a moment like this? There are no words. Holding back tears so as not to upset the kids, who were staying with her, Mom said insistently: "You know that you are my everything." And to assure me the kids would be cared for, she added, "I've got this."

I said to her, *You need to be OK,* and hung up the phone.

At 7 a.m. Denny was awakened by a call from the surgeon telling him I was in recovery, my body critically infected. A second call, as Denny was preparing to leave for the hospital, was more foreboding. He was asked to meet with Dr. Syed Anees, a respirologist and attending physician of the ICU, at 9 a.m.

Denny described it as his own gut punch. "Oh God, what happened?"

Dr. Anees was joined in the quiet room by Rosemary Hogan-Kobrynovich, a counsellor who was known to my mother through her professional network, and other members of the medical team, to share the diagnosis. He was grim-faced. He said I was in septic shock.

"It's really bad. There is a high level of infection in her abdomen and a large number of abscesses. We are doing all we can."

Septic shock? Denny cut to the chase: "How bad is 'really bad?' What are the percentages?"

"At her level of infection, less than a 40-per-cent survival rate. Honestly, I can't tell you because I don't know how her body's going to react. She is on antibiotics and we cleaned it up the best we could."

How I managed to go into septic shock, one day after being discharged from hospital, is a mystery I have yet to solve.

According to the Mayo Clinic, sepsis is a potentially life-threatening condition that occurs when the body's response to an infection goes out of whack, attacking its own tissues. When the infection-fighting processes turn on the body, they cause organs to function poorly and abnormally. Septic shock is a severe, potentially lethal drop in blood pressure that results in highly abnormal problems with how cells work and produce energy.

An estimated 18,000 Canadians die from sepsis each year, according to Health Canada.

Sepsis is such a threat in critical care units that the Mayo has developed a "sepsis sniffer" to help detect it in patients at higher risk. A specialized team uses technology to monitor things such as fever, heart rate and blood pressure, receiving a warning when conditions are ripe for an attack.

My parents were exploding with emotion. Their lives were spent preparing for me to die before them. And now that it was happening, their preparation was for naught. Mom estimates she supported 800 parents as a bereavement counsellor, and now the roles were reversed. The family was advised to call in my brothers, Craig and Kenny, for reasons not specified but clearly understood. It might be their last time to see me alive.

In the quiet room, which was all too familiar to my mother, she proceeded to fling a table and four chairs aside, creating a space on the floor where she lay face-down and prayed, "Please don't take her away from her babies. Please let them have their mother." The act of prostration is part of the Good Friday liturgy, a symbol of surrender to God's will. Mom says that once she prostrated herself, a calm descended on her that would remain throughout my hospital ordeal. She felt like a protective veil had been placed over her.

Mom requested a priest so he could perform a viaticum, or anointing of the sick, which is more commonly referred to as last rites. Mom, Dad and Rosemary, the counsellor, held hands at my bedside while the prayers were quietly spoken. He anointed me with oil, blessed me and forgave my sins.

In a conscious moment, I told my mother: *Do everything to save me, no matter how drastic. I have three little ones and a husband who needs and loves me.*

I am told that my condition worsened. Quickly. My white blood cells continued on their rampage. Another emergency surgery was performed at my hospital bed because my condition was too compromised to move me to a surgical suite.

At that point, what needed to be done, could not be done with me conscious. Denny was allowed to see me in the ICU one last time before I was placed in a medically induced coma and on life support. He squeezed my hand and whispered in my ear, "I love you." And then he was excused from the room. I needed to be comatose so my body could focus on fighting the infection. It would stop me from wrestling with the ventilator that would breathe for me.

Earlier that day I made my final Facebook post for nearly a month, and to this day, I don't remember pressing the keys.

The fluids being pumped into me to flush out the infection caused my body mass to balloon. My weight doubled to more than 200 pounds and I became unrecognizable to my family. Denny said my torso looked like an oversized water balloon, my hands like inflated Latex gloves. My neck was no longer circular, rather, it appeared to flow directly from head to shoulders like an underinflated beach ball. Picture Jabba the Hutt from Star Wars.

Denny, overwhelmed, had to leave the room during last rites. In the hallway Rosemary offered him a glass of water and whatever encouragement she could muster. He told her he needed time alone.

Denny believes in a higher power and the afterlife but is not wedded to a particular faith like my mom. In fact, he found the constant entreaties to pray annoying. Pray to whom? Does the Holy Spirit rank higher than the Father and Son, and if so, why doesn't he/she reach down and save my wife? He thought the petitions to God represented a form of surrender. The notion that I was being lost, he felt, was defeatist.

He is the most spiritual yet anti-religious person I know.

For her part, and despite the awful things that happened to her daughter, my mother's faith was unwavering. She mused about having a discussion with God about this turmoil, but otherwise persevered.

Colleen Dufour Campo is with **Danielle Campo McLeod** and **41 others**.

September 9, 2021 · 🌐

•••

Please light a candle …. Put it outside, on your table, anywhere - light up this city for Danielle. Just went through surgery number 4 - just trying to keep her here. We need the energy of love and light. Please pray for my girl. JESUS I TRUST IN YOU

 Colleen Dufour Campo is with **Danielle Campo McLeod** and **8 others**.

September 9, 2021 · 🌐

•••

 ## Pray we are loosing heR. PRAY NOW

😢💙😥 416   571 Comments 22 Shares

 Colleen Dufour Campo

September 9, 2021 · 🌐

•••

 ## Out of surgery. ICU …. So very scared.

😢💙👍 121   69 Comments 1 Share

 Colleen Dufour Campo is with **Danielle Campo McLeod** and **7 others**.

September 9, 2021 · 🌐

•••

Going back in surgery….. DEAR GOD I BEG YOU TO HOLD HER IN YOUR ARMS. I KNOW YOU ARE

 😢💙👍 Carlo Abati and 304 others   188 Comments 1 Share

When they saw me, my brothers were gobsmacked. They muttered, "What. The. Fuck?" They stood at my bedside, transfixed by the machines monitoring my blood pressure, heart rate and oxygen levels. "Watching these stupid machines," Denny said, "hoping for the numbers to go up." But they didn't. Everything was mind-numbingly stagnant.

Thinking of the kids I would leave motherless, Craig half-jokingly asked the surgeon if he could trade places with me. "I only have a cat," he said.

Kenny returned one day with a vial of blessed oil from Ste. Anne de Beaupré, a renowned pilgrimage destination in Quebec. A Hindu faith healer blessed some water which Mom smuggled into the hospital in a used plastic bottle, in violation of COVID rules, and stashed behind a curtain in my room. I was literally basted with healing liquids on a daily basis – over my heart, on my feet. Wherever the spirit moved Mom.

My brothers Craig and Kenny have always been my protectors

Denny told me the first days of my coma were the "longest, most agonizing" in his life. Denny was the decision-maker in my family support unit, constantly conferring with the medical teams as they exhausted repeated attempts to thwart the infection and restore my blood pressure.

They tried a treatment called IVIG (intravenous immune globulin) to help my body counter the infection with antibodies. I was covered in ice, from head to toe, to help with the fever.

At one point, Denny signed an authorization for doctors to inject me with Methylene Blue, a drug used to treat methemoglobinemia, the blood's inability to deliver oxygen through the body. Doctors hoped it would open my veins to assist the five different IV medications, or pressors, fighting the blood pressure drop. It was a Hail Mary. When Denny asked what they thought, my family replied, "What do we have to lose?" It was my expressed wish to take extraordinary measures.

Hope was dimming and the words my family lived by, "Oh, it's Danielle, she's tough, she'll pull through," were losing credibility. Everyone was on edge. My brothers were angry – visibly and vocally – that things had reached this point.

The media began to report on my crisis: The little blond pixie whose swimming exploits put us on the map needs the favour returned. It was the talk of dinner tables across the region and reached a global audience via social media.

My family received hundreds of posts and emails from home and abroad, many from people offering diapers, food and toys for the kids. Because we had no room to store the donations in our house, Denny set up a GoFundMe campaign to help with the expenses that would, hopefully, be needed in my long recovery.

A friend from my childhood, Terri Gagnon, wanted to help in a way that transcended money. Our fathers met shortly after they emigrated from Europe – Terri's from Poland and mine from Italy – and bonded during street hockey games. The only English they knew at the time was, "Shoot puck like you can."

When Terri read my mother's "pray now we're losing her" post, and despite her nearly crippling shyness, she went on Facebook live to launch a virtual prayer group. Each night at 8:30 she rallied followers to pray for me. Within days the site reached 1,500 followers, hundreds of them showing up seven nights a week. When I wrote this memoir, they were still praying for my complete recovery and other worthy causes ranging from a cancer patient to the victim of a motorcycle crash.

Healing prayers for
Danielle
Campo-McLeod

Mahee Munasinghe, the Hindu faith healer who had blessed water for us, contacted my mother-in-law Linda about the power of intention-based candles, lit in the home as part of traditional ceremonies known as Havans. She said the candles would conjure healing powers for a sick loved one and the power would endure only as long as the candle remained lit. Mom borrowed a candle from my neighbour and placed it in our kitchen sink. While it was later moved to a less conspicuous location, it would not be extinguished as long as I was in the hospital. Mahee spent an entire day praying for me on the steps of Assumption Church.

Candles were lit – physically or virtually – across the region and beyond. A man who had heard me speak years ago, and for whom I autographed a scrap paper with the message, "Never give up," sent a photo of it to Denny, saying I needed it more than he did. Many wanted me to know they had stopped praying, until word of my plight compelled them to start again.

A neighbour supplied my household with home-baked goodies while I was laid up, saying, "When you open this door the love that comes out of this house, I just need to feel it." Managing the chaos of our household fell to my in-laws Linda and Allan. Linda prepared and managed an agenda for the many who stepped up to help with the kids. They grocery shopped, entertained the boys and managed the many lasagna dinners dropped off at our place. In our absence, our siblings and their spouses gave the kids all the love and support they would have received from us.

Denny's artist friend Alison Dilworth was working on a wall mural in Philadelphia, a massive floral artwork 111 feet long. It was titled, Dark is a Way and Light is a place. She dedicated a lily to me.

My spirits were lifted by the messages, texts, photographs and posts my mother shared with me. Here's an example:

Tracy Simpson

September 10, 2021 · 🌐

I am sharing this post to ask for your help in send healing thoughts to one of the most inspirational young ladies I know.

I met Danielle 20 years ago through my work at Muscular Dystrophy Canada. She was 16, a Paralympian who won many medals in swimming and an amazing role model for young and old alike. Having been diagnosed at a young age with Muscular Dystrophy, she faced daily battles and had to overcome many challenges.

My family was called in a second time to say their goodbyes. Everyone but Denny joined in. He swore to never say goodbye.

The hospital was a miserable place full of COVID coughing and lonely patients who had no one to comfort them due to pandemic restrictions. My mother approached the nursing station directly across from my room and pronounced, "You need to hear what I'm saying," which got the medical team's attention. What she said brought many of them to tears.

"I need you to save her. But if you can't, you need to know we're going to be OK. So I don't want you thinking that you failed us. You give it everything because there are three little babies at home. I know you've been through so much. But just do this. You've got to save her."

Denny had a different view. "Fuck her," he said. "We wouldn't be OK."

A medical treatment that is good for one organ isn't necessarily good for another. The ordeal was placing enormous strain on my heart. It was failing. If the sepsis didn't kill me, a heart attack might. Dr. Anees made a crucial decision to transfer me to University Hospital in London, home of a more advanced cardiac department. Yes, a patient in an induced coma and covered in IVs would be transported 200 km away.

I had a 10 per cent chance to survive the journey.

Take Everything I Have

Dr. Anees gathered my family around the nursing station. He had a soothing way about him that reminded my family of a morning dew: Kind eyes and the gentlest hands. His graceful gait gave the appearance of floating in and out of a room. Aided by two interns, he had been working the phones feverishly to get a transfer approved by the six medical disciplines, ranging from cardiac care to infectious disease, required to treat me at University Hospital. My family put its faith in him.

He said if we didn't leave Windsor, I had no chance to survive. He asked: "Do you want to spend her remaining time here, saying goodbye? Because we are losing her." What he described, according to my mother, sounded like palliative care. At least with the London option, I had a 10 per cent chance of making it. "Time to go down the 401," he said.

A plan to fly me on the province's Ornge Air Ambulance was scuttled. The helipad at University Hospital was out of service. Landing elsewhere would mean a series of lengthy, dangerous transfers. Dr. Anees said no. Too much risk. It was decided that Ornge's ground ambulance would transport me.

With all the gadgets and gizmos keeping me alive, it took two hours to prep me for the trip. Two hours for the anxiety to build in Denny. When it was time to go, he squeezed my hand, closed his eyes and in a trembling voice, said, "You take as much strength from me as you need. And you FUCKING MAKE THIS TRIP. I'm giving you everything I have. Just *take it*." He kissed me on the forehead and said he would see me in London. And as he packed a bag for his trip down the highway, he repeated to himself, "She's going to make it. She's going to make it. She *has* to make it."

It's a wonder he kept his Jeep between the lines of the 401. An emotional wreck, in his words "a prisoner in my own mind," he refused to accept that there was a 90 per cent chance his wife would not survive the trip.

By the time I left Windsor Regional Hospital, he was halfway to London, sitting at a rest stop waiting for a call, unable to slow his racing mind. "We're not ending like this. It's not happening. I just refuse to accept it. Even if it did happen, I would still refuse to accept that she didn't make it. Not an option for me."

With my blood pressure still perilously low, Dr. Anees was not taking chances. Although it is not standard protocol, he jumped into the ambulance to accompany me for the trip. And that decision, I believe, saved my life. While we were in transit, he communicated to the hospital my complicated life-support setup, providing the information needed to plug me into the care system at University. I'm told he called the hospital nearly 20 times.

My treatment at Windsor Regional, between Aug. 17 and Sept. 7, was a mashup of medical disciplines ranging from obstetrics to gastroenterology. My file consisted of more than 2,000 medical records. The cocktail of paralytics that was maintaining my coma, in and of itself, was mind-boggling. Without Dr. Anees at my side, I don't know how the paramedics would have coped with unforeseen developments on the road. I wonder if they've ever transported someone in my condition.

Denny and my parents were allowed to wait in the entrance of University Hospital in spite of COVID regulations, and when the ambulance pulled in, miraculous, Mom thought, she almost keeled over in relief. Since Denny never entertained the idea that I might die on the highway, his response was more muted. He was all about the business of saving my life.

Thanks to Dr. Anees's intervention, a hospital admission that would normally take two hours took 20 minutes.

I arrived in London with an obscenely high white blood cell count and was listed in critical condition. Thankfully, transitioning into the University Hospital ecosystem was seamless. A team of what seemed like 20 specialists, nurses and attendants was prepped to tackle my complex case. My family took comfort when one of them, Dr. Matthew Valdis, introduced himself. He was the aspiring cardiologist who took me to the high school prom in Grade 11.

He said to my parents, "I want you to know that we are going to do everything to get your daughter better. And also, Mr. Campo, I have to apologize. I took two beers from your fridge when we were 17 years old, and your daughter and I went to my prom."

Laughter broke the tension and Denny quipped, "She could have married a cardiologist. Great. Just great." Mom posted, "God keeps showing us his presence... in the hands of someone who knows how incredible Danielle is."

The slow process of fighting the infection while maintaining my blood pressure played out over weeks. Doctors began to reduce the paralytic drugs to prepare for waking me from the coma. My angel of mercy, this time, was an ICU nurse named Jody. She held my hand and told me I would be OK. She bent the hospital rules to allow Denny to take up residence on the floor. She approached setbacks with a sense of humour, proclaiming, when my ostomy bag failed, "Well, that's a shit disaster."

All the while, the community continued to rally behind me, in spirit and in cash. Donors boosted the GoFundMe campaign to more than $90,000 and London firefighters committed to paying for my family's living expenses.

My mother received a message from philanthropist Rick Hansen, Canada's foremost advocate for athletes with disabilities and founder of the Man In Motion World Tour. My best friend, Courtney Stearns, drove to London with a lit candle in her front seat so she could meditate in the hospital parking lot outside my window.

On Sept. 14, Denny, calling it "the best day I've had in a week," reported that in my comatose state I was able to gently grab his hand. "I always knew she was strong," he said, "but this is a whole new level." He predicted I would be off the ventilator within days.

"I can't wait to look you in the eyes again baby. We aren't out of the woods, but I feel we are on a path and on our way."

Confessions Of A Comatose Mind

Scene 1: I'm swimming laps in preparation for the Paralympics and my training partners, Adam and Benoit, are screaming at me. I'm so tired. But each time I try to leave the pool they scream louder: "You've got to keep going! You can't stop! Quit counting your laps and just swim, Danielle." My coach is yelling at me too. "You've got to get your heart rate up! Swim hard!" But I am so tired. I just want to leave the pool. And I want to know, why is everyone being so bossy?

Scene 2: Denny is driving on the highway and falling asleep at the wheel. I am both inside the car and staring in from the outside. "Wake up! You need to wake up and get out of the car!" He doesn't wake up. He crashes. (Postscript: 25 years ago, Denny fell asleep at the wheel and crashed.)

Scene 3: I'm sitting by a fire with my Uncle Rich. I call him Big Dude. We talk a lot about important things. "Danielle, you need to go and live your passion," he says. *I don't know what you mean? I'm passionate.* "No, I'm talking about living your passion. No more just doing passion. I want you to live it." I say, *Of course Big Dude. That's what I do.* And he says, "It's time to change it. Go now and live it stop doing it." *OK Big Dude.* (Postscript: Big Dude passed away years before Morgan was born.)

Scene 4: I walk into a farmhouse where my grandparents are playing cards. They are at a table with other relatives whose faces are blurred. I ask to sit at the table like I have done many times as a child. Pepe says, "There are no chairs for you." I ask him to sneak me some of the cheese they are eating, another childhood ritual. He says, "You can't eat this food." *What the heck? Pepe I just need a chair.* He shakes his head. "There's nowhere for you to sit here." My grandmother isn't helping. She's not even acknowledging me. She invites everyone but me to go dancing. I think, *Why is everybody being so rude?*

Scene 5: I climb a narrow flight of stairs to a bedroom where a beautiful baby named Stephanie is laying in a crib. She is wearing a red velvet dress. I scoop her up and rock her in my arms, humming a lullaby. She's barely a year old but carries on a conversation with me as if she is much older. She says, "You can pick me up and rock me until you get back to Morgan. I'm OK. And you're going to be OK." In her presence I feel an overwhelming calm, my maternal instincts kicking in as if I was rocking my own newborn. (Postscript: My second cousin Audrey's daughter, Stephanie, died in childhood. Audrey takes comfort in knowing that Stephanie is OK.)

Scene 6: I'm in a dark room and an object appears in front of me. It is a round hairbrush with a wooden handle. I recognize the brush from childhood when I would play with Grandfather Campo's hair. When I reach out to grab the hairbrush a loud voice, my Nono's, yells out, "Do not touch the hairbrush!" I freeze, like in a horror movie when a ghost appears. *Don't look behind you and don't look in front of you. Stay exactly where you are.* I'm not frightened. Suddenly, thousands of lights come on, illuminating a path in front of me. And the voice says, "You can go this way."

Scene 7: I'm talking to my mother in my hospital room. It's pitch dark. Mom says she will never leave my side; I am her everything. Take small breaths and little steps, she says, and we will get through this together. "You just need to keep trusting in God. He's got this. He's healing you." (Postcript: When I awoke, the first thing my mother said is, "You just need to keep trusting in God. He's got this. He's healing you.")

Scene 8: I'm in a classroom talking to Corbin's teacher. I tell her she must take care of him until he graduates. She says yes. "I'm not leaving this school." I turn to Corbin, who is sitting on my lap. *Corbin, mummy is too sick, and I need to go to Heaven now. My body is just too sick. I can't do it anymore. So I'm gonna go. I know I promised you that I'd come back but I can't. Mommy has to go to Heaven.* (Postscript: Shortly after I awakened, Corbin told me this story: "Yeah Mommy, you walked into my room, I sat up and you said your body was too sick. You had to go to Heaven. And I was mad at you because you promised you were going to come home. I hugged you and said, 'Please don't go Mommy.'" The next thing he knew, Denny was in the room telling him that I opened my eyes.)

Scene 9: I'm walking down a beach and a little girl with curly blond hair is coming out of the water, laughing. She is wearing a pink dress and looks like me at the time I was diagnosed with muscular dystrophy. I'm trying to catch up to her. I feel a maternal connection to her. She turns to me and says, "This place is great. You're gonna love this place. But not yet." And then she disappears into the water. (Postscript: Between the births of our sons, Denny and I lost a child to an ectopic pregnancy.)

Scene 10: I am having tea with Denny's cousin Sarah, my soul sister with whom I share a special connection. I promise her I will return to my body but it is too sick at this time. We are planning to start a wellness business. I tell her if I can't make it back she must promise that she will carry on our healing work.

Scene 11: My naturopathic specialist is screaming at the doctors to stop the antibiotics and "wash out her body." They put me through what feels like a carwash. And the infection is gone.

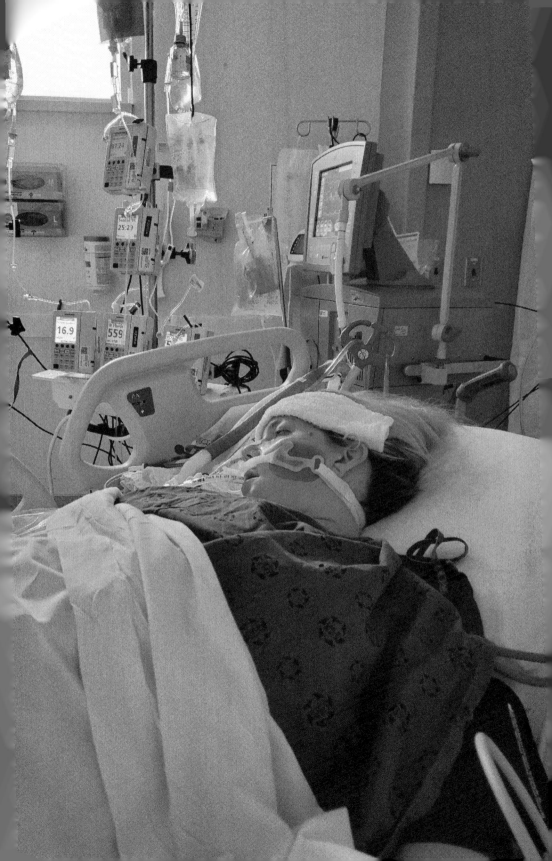

Awakening

"Hi. I'm Dennis. But everyone calls me Denny."

My husband was introducing himself to an ICU nurse when his voice pierced the veil of my coma. My eyes flung open. I was back. Disoriented beyond words, but back.

Denny burst into tears at the sight of my awakening. He raced to my bedside and gently squeezed my hand.

"I waited so long to see those eyes."

Emotions overwhelmed him and for the first time since I went comatose seven days earlier, he allowed hope to creep in. The symphony of sounds from the ventilator, the dozen IV poles, the odd smells and muffled voices, the dread of more bad news, faded to the background in that instant.

What was it like emerging from a coma? Imagine waking from the most blissfully peaceful nap, only to find that your body is not working. It feels like you are encased in cement from head to toe. Nothing moves. And your memory is gone.

In those eyes he so desperately wanted to open, Denny saw something foreign: fear.

What happened to me?

Did we get into a car accident?

Why. Am. I. Paralyzed?

Noticeably absent from those questions was, what happened to our baby? But I had no recollection – zero – of her birth. Two boys and two stepchildren? I had no recollection of them either.

I was convinced that my worst fear since childhood had come true: Not

110

a single muscle in my body was working. Memories of those frightening trips to the specialists, to check off the latest organ malfunction, came flooding back. Had my body raised the white flag?

Denny, talk to me!

In the three minutes he was allotted before nurses tossed him to change my dressing, and with nurse Jody standing guard, Denny was necessarily patient and selective with the answers so as not to overwhelm me.

"I got a lot to tell you. But we're gonna take it really slowly. I know you're not happy about that because you want answers right now."

He assured me I was not paralyzed. *Thank God!* As the paralytic drugs wore off, he said, my muscles would start working again. "You went into septic shock. You had to go to London. But you're doing way better."

I was freaked out by my inability to breathe on my own. As I counted the readings on the vent to keep from panicking, he cheered me with news of the world rallying behind me and the hundreds of candles – virtual and otherwise – that were lit on my behalf.

"Danielle, you have no idea what's going on back home. So many people supporting you. I'm getting messages from people in France and South Africa. Prayer vigils every night. It's crazy the way the community has rallied. It's exploding."

He did not mention our newborn daughter. Too much baggage associated with that one.

And then, his three minutes were up and I went back to the business of recovery. I had significant mountains to climb. Not only would the medical team wean me off paralytics, but I would learn to breathe without the ventilator. My blood pressure remained an issue. And there was the ruthless invader sepsis. It had not gone away. All this while saddled with a neuromuscular disorder.

The process played out like a well-orchestrated stage production as doctors lowered the percentage of breathing that the vent did on my behalf. I made it easier for them as my inner Olympian came out. The vent became another success metric, like a stopwatch. The sound it made conjured up the clicking of a training snorkel. By focusing on my breathing and pushing my lungs to their limit, I challenged myself to move the dials ever higher. Each day I reached a new peak, prompting one physician to remark, "Danielle, you are the first person I've ever seen to work out while on life-support."

"Most people who come off the vent will need sedation, but you look like you just spent a week on the beach."

The psychological recovery would also take time. One day, Denny and I were trying to communicate with an alphabet sheet because the vent prevented me from speaking. He taped a tongue depressor to my finger so I could point out the letters. I tapped out, *I need to tell you. Do not give up on me.*

My husband laughed, saying, "If I haven't given up by now, there's no chance I'll ever give up on you."

Getting me off the vent was a delicate dance. For days, they tweaked the settings to increase the percentage of room air, only to pull back when my readings were poor. Because of my neuromuscular disorder, my lung capacity was less than a person without a disability. I tried to convey to them that my baseline lung capacity was 70 per cent, not 100 per cent.

My eyes were screaming, *If I'm at 70 per cent, it is my normal. Get this thing out!*

I thought my doctor's decision to pull the tube was courageous given the uncertainty over my lung capacity. She told a cluster of med students that we were at a critical stage of my recovery. If I didn't get off the vent soon, my organs could deteriorate. When my parents asked about worst-case scenarios, she said that if the removal failed, the vent would be re-inserted.

Screw that, I thought. *Once that sucker is out, it is not going back in.*

The removal was set for a Sunday. Denny went home the day before to spend time with the kids. When it came to my milestones, his timing had always been bad and this one was no exception. Doctors decided the vent would come out on Saturday when he was 200 km away.

A nurse with a thick European accent came in to check on my readiness. I summoned all my strength to produce a convincing grunt. She looked me in the eye and asked, "You want to come off of this? You want us to try?" I gave her a big thumbs up.

Unaware that she was treating a former competitive swimmer, she said, "It's going to feel like you're drowning. But if you want to pull it, we can pull it now."

Swimmer. Drowning. Right.

They told me to cough and keep coughing. But with no strength, my first attempt was pathetic. A flaccid *ehh*. The tube was pulled and guess what, it did feel like I was drowning. I struggled for every ounce of oxygen. It was like trying to breathe through a tiny straw with someone plugging the tip.

I pulled something out of my bag of swimming tricks: Hypoxic training. It's how we were taught to cope with reduced oxygen by taking short "trickle breaths." Puff. Puff. Puff. The technique allows swimmers to take more strokes between breaths.

I repeated to myself, *You'll get your breath of air when you get to the wall.*

All the while I focused on maintaining my composure, another swimming specialty, because if I freaked you, they would re-insert the vent. I pretended not to freak out. Meanwhile I thought, *Oh my God, this is horrible!* But I was so desperate to speak again – to actually confirm that I *could make words come out of my mouth* – that nothing was stopping me. I uttered a barely audible *Hi* to my parents, in a voice so distorted that it rattled my dad.

"Is this normal?" he asked the nurse. My Eastern European angel winked at me. "Yes, your daughter is winning."

Nurse Jody cried when she returned from vacation to find me off the vent, her impossibly long blond mane drooping out of its ponytail. "You're my good news story," she said.

My father cried too. I said in a fine whisper, *You really need to toughen up Dad.*

Try as he might, Dad kept doing things that irritated me. And in my post-coma state I was easily irritated. My family called it my "barky stage." One day, Dad was jangling the coins in his pocket so loudly that I thought my ears would explode. When I told him to stop he scooped up the change and hurled it into the windowsill.

"I'm going for coffee," he declared.

He returned moments later, head down, empty-handed.

***

At their peak, IV tubes were pumping 44 medications into my veins. Drug regimens were constantly tweaked to fight the infection, maintain my blood pressure and protect my heart. To keep track of the complex treatment, Denny leaned on his buddy Ryan Lucier, a critical care nurse, and my cousin Lisa Pozzobon, a respiratory therapist. The peace of mind they gave him caused the nurses to label Denny the "calmest, saddest person" they had ever seen.

My mother posted a jarring photo of the dozen IV machines keeping me alive through five bowel surgeries in two days.

One night, the bizarro world of my coma dreams met its match in the mother of all hallucinations – one that would threaten my life once again.

I had not slept in three days. It was 3 a.m. and I was burning with fever. Suddenly and inexplicably, Uncle Leo, founder of the Campo bun fight, appeared in my hospital room, declaring, "The doctor says I can take these off of you." He pointed to the tubes and gadgets that were keeping me alive. "I'll get them all off."

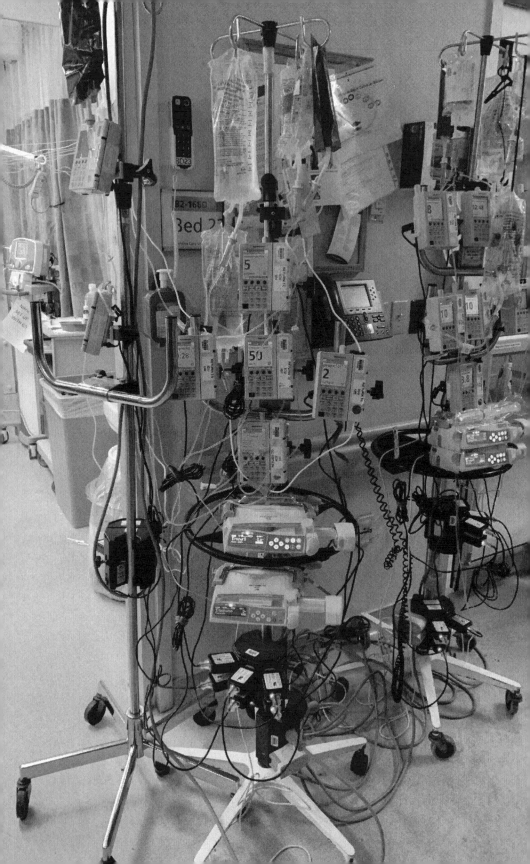

My brothers appeared, telling me to jump out the hospital window. (Figures! An old bun-fight tactic!)

My son's teacher showed up. I told her that I was going to die, that I needed to go to Heaven and that I had failed to take care of my child.

Uncle Leo persisted. "Let's take all those things off of you."

Ever the obedient niece, I proceeded to pull every tube out of my body. Also, the vacuum which was sucking infection from my abdomen, the ostomy bag, the feeding tube and my heart monitor.

The heart monitor's disconnection set off an alarm, sending all seven floor nurses flying to my room. They found me lying there, tubeless.

"What did you do?" one exclaimed. "You could have pulled your entire bowel out!"

My fog shrouded response was: *I'm all done. I'm all done. Thanks. I'm all done.*

When he arrived at 6 a.m., Denny found me trussed in patient restraints, a sea of straps.

"Rough night, eh?"

I felt the need to apologize to my nurse. *I'm really sorry, I gave you a run for your money there. You were probably on your break.* The nurse, unaccustomed to patients apologizing for near-death experiences, replied, "You give me the hope I need to keep doing this. You need to get better."

When my fog lifted, I was gripped by a new fear: What happens when I don't have a team of nurses and specialists, and their sophisticated equipment, monitoring my every heartbeat. The day was coming soon.

But despite my Uncle Leo episode, I was anxious to be liberated from University Hospital. I didn't equivocate with the medical team. I wanted out by Oct. 30. I will be home, with my kids, in time to trick-or-treat, I vowed. And it was not negotiable. Give me a firm date. Give me that goal. Put it up on a board and I promise you I will beat it. And I will beat it by two weeks.

Because that is what I do.

Reluctantly, because they wanted to manage my expectations, the doctor set Oct. 31 as the target to release me into a rehabilitation centre in Windsor. I wasn't fussy about spending time at another way station on my road home but, thankfully, agreed to rehab. "As long as you promise not to eat too much candy," she said, "you will be home on Halloween."

By that time, 44 days would have passed since my daughter's birth.

My recovery would not be easy. A CT scan showed five abscesses in my abdomen which were harboring infection. They were not in a position to be drained, so the infectious-disease team needed to develop a kick-ass antibiotic regimen.

I struggled mentally but was rescued by my nurses' compassionate care. Jody talked to me like a BFF, not a patient. Having her put up my hair was a dream. Another nurse placed an iPad at the foot of my bed with tropical fish on the screen. She massaged my scalp, saying that when she did it for her children, it soothed them.

On Sept. 20 I consumed my first solid food – chocolate pudding – in more than a month. The following day I was transferred to the medical surgery floor to build my strength, telling my mom, in a voice reminiscent of Amy Winehouse after a two-hour concert, I *... had ... a ... busy ... day.* I could move my fingers, but not my arms or legs. I could turn my head but not lift it. Pushing my glasses up my nose was a milestone accomplishment. Because my normal state was diminished by a neuromuscular disorder, the recovery from a coma took longer.

My mom posted, "Each day I watch her excruciatingly work on getting stronger. The doctors say she truly has that athlete spirit."

Mom tried to soothe me with music for my earbuds. She loaded up the Enya, mistaking me for a fan of the folksy Irish songstress. Denny rescued me with alt bands he knew I liked: Manchester Orchestra, Bear's Den and Lord Huron. Surprised to find me sitting up in a chair one morning, Denny posted, "She's pushing herself to recover. Every day she is doing more and more."

I started to have trouble clearing my lungs, earning me a return to the ICU where I received added attention from nurses, a physiotherapist and a respirologist. I had forgotten that excessive saliva was a side-effect of Mestinon, which I had resumed. It explained why a simple cough took all the strength I could muster. Mom asked the nightly prayer vigil to focus on healing my lungs.

Mestinon, the drug that had change my life, was relegated to the bench once again. My breathing problems were resolved but I would never again take it.

One morning during a sponge bath, I noticed milk leaking from my breasts. I burst into tears because it was the first time I realized that I had a newborn. Yes, septic shock can do that to your memory. It was a devastating blow, what I consider the lowest moment of my life. *I have a baby. And I haven't even met her.*

What's more, I had two other kids at home, and Denny's two. I had abandoned them. My mind was an inferno of guilt and worry. *Oh God, where are they sleeping? What are they eating?*

At this moment I had nothing left internally to pull from and the nurses

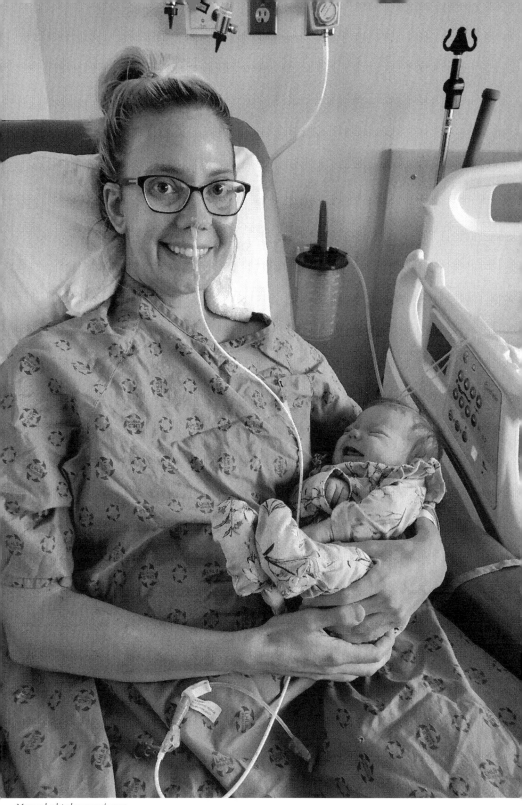

Morgan back in her mama's arms

became my lifeline. Admitting that my tank was dry was the first time in my life that I said I can't do this, and it was OK to say "can't." It did not mean I was giving up, nor that I wasn't strong enough. It simply meant that in this moment I needed others to carry the fight for me.

As my head crashed back into the pillow, Denny walked in. I said to him I have children and I need to be with them. *I can't do this anymore.* Denny reminded me I was not doing this for me. I was doing this for the five children who needed me. I was doing this for the husband who needed a wife by his side. I was doing this for the entire community that was finding hope in my fight. Moving me to a private room helped bring about a mindset change, of not focusing on what I can't do or where I can't be. I focused on what others could do for me that would recharge my internal reservoir. My strength hadn't left; it was simply inaccessible in that moment.

The nurses told Denny that for the sake of my mental health, he needed to bring Morgan to the hospital. Denny was saddened by my reaction but thankful that I had finally been awakened about our children.

The wait for her arrival was gut-wrenching, like giving birth all over again. Mom stood at my window overlooking the parking lot to deliver a play-by-play of Denny pulling into the parking lot and removing Morgan from her red car seat. The nurses formed an honour guard to welcome them to my room. Morgan flashed a big smile as if to say, "I'm the star of the show."

I wasn't strong enough to hold her, so Denny placed her in my lap and the nurses entwined my fingers under her bottom. It pleased me that she hadn't developed the strength to hold her head upright – at least I hadn't missed that milestone. She had a strawberry birthmark on the bridge of her nose. She was so much smaller than I expected. And prettier. I had given birth to a little doll.

When she locked eyes with Denny it was clear to me that they had bonded. He couldn't be out of her sight without her bursting into tears. He was her safety net. I was not.

I felt a flicker of maternal instinct, wondering why they had dressed her in ruffles for a long ride in a car seat. I tried to give her a bottle but lacked the strength. I cradled her in my arms and sang her my favourite lullaby from children's author Robert Munsch.

I'll love you forever,
I'll like you for always,
As long as I'm living
My baby you'll be.

Except, in my version the third line was: *I promise I'll be living.*

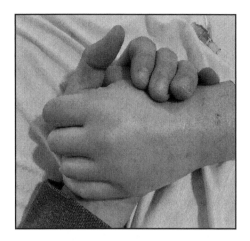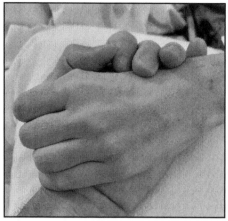

The visit was a godsend. In my infant child I found strength and inspiration. I was more determined than ever to reunite with my family. I thought: *Now I know what I'm fighting for.* I said to Denny, *Holy shit, we have five kids!*

I continued to make progress. Denny snapped photographs of my hands on consecutive days to illustrate the diminished swelling. "Fluids are finally leaving her body. Great to see her returning to shape and having more energy."

My lifelines to the outside world began to return. I had been doing Facetime video with my niece and nephew, Leelan and Aria, throughout the ordeal. Until this time, the sight of me caused Leelan to be inconsolable. Now able to face me, he said, "You're looking like you again Aunt Danielle. You're going to make it."

Mom started to notice a change in me. Not only was my body recovering, but I had a better grasp of the magnitude of my ordeal. I was deeply thankful for the medical teams who devoted their lives to this cause. I struggled for the words to express my gratitude to Mom, Dad, Linda and Allan for helping Denny care for the kids. I was in awe of the love and support they received from friends and total strangers. I said: *I am so grateful for the people who have held me so tight.*

I told my mother that while I was reluctant to close my eyes, for fear they may not open again, *I am going to come back stronger... just wait and see.* It took me seven days of practice to finally pass the swallowing assessment so I could eat regular food. My first sip of water since coming to the ICU made me joyful and I told my mom that I was going to order steak and lobster for my first hospital meal. Denny's bad luck persisted – he was home with the kids when I passed my swallowing test.

Days were filled with physio, speech therapy, dietitians, nurses, doctors, social workers and personal support staff. I spent more time with Morgan.

On Oct. 1, I was scheduled for a procedure to drain the abscesses so the infectious-disease team could culture them. The hope remained to rid them from my body with antibiotics, not surgery. The prep alone was tedious and painful Change my dressing. Remove the vac machine. Remove the IVs. Cry out in pain when they move me from the bed to a stretcher. Watch tears stream down my cheek when I said goodbye to Morgan.

I looked my mother in the eye: *Promise me I will be OK.*

Denny was the even keel that I needed in this moment. "Try not to get frustrated; stay patient. We'll take the good with the not so good and keep rolling along. Take the time to heal, Danielle. We are here for you."

I emerged from the procedure with a pleasant surprise for Denny and Mom: My feeding tube was removed. I could stand up. I took four steps and burst into tears.

I am going to walk again!

I progressed to 30 steps, then 100, finally getting outside to eat lunch in a courtyard with Denny. I missed my children terribly and arrangements were made for me to Facetime with the boys. Feeling particularly daring, I took to Facebook Live to report another milestone: Taking my first steps without a walker. The hospital corridor was my Olympic track.

I looked at the calendar on my wall and realized that Morgan was two months old. Ouch. It hurt to think of everything I missed. I allowed myself to briefly feel the sadness then turned my attention to how blessed I was to have my parents and in-laws care for my children. I walked one loop of my Olympic track for each of my kids.

On the eve of a CT scan that would tell me if I could go home, I was optimistic because my feverishness had diminished as the antibiotics did their work. After the scan I heard my doctor's footsteps in the hallway. He leaned against the wall and placed his hand on his hip, a serious pose that made me worry, *Shit, it's bad news, right?*

He looked me in the eye and said, "It is better than a best-case scenario Danielle. And now I gotta give you a hug. You have zero sign of infection."

Danielle Campo McLeod
October 18, 2021 · 🌐

· · ·

I'm Coming Home!!!!!!!!!!!

⭕💙😮 884   201 Comments 51 Shares

A Pinterest Mom Doesn't Poop in a Bag

After more than a month relying on machines to keep me alive, I felt like an astronaut on a spacewalk. My tether was about to be cut. Think George Clooney floating aimlessly in the sci-fi thriller Gravity. I was terrified. On the night before my release from University Hospital, nurses unhooked me and I panicked. I imagined my stomach was about to explode. I labored to breathe. Convinced I was having a heart attack. I pressed the call button.

"It's just anxiety," a nurse said. "It's totally normal. You've been hooked up to machines keeping you alive for so long."

Any doubt about spending two weeks in a rehab centre was erased. I needed this time to heal, physically and emotionally. I needed to learn to change the ostomy bag that would serve as my surrogate bowels until, hopefully, I could have the ileostomy reversed. Thankfully, Denny spent hours watching nurses tend to the bag so, sorry for your luck Den, you will be my Minister of Poop.

In the medical transport on my way home, the paramedic was oddly quiet. I was hoping for someone chattier to make the time pass quickly. She seemed fixated on some written reports which turned out to be my medical records. From time to time she whispered, "Oh my goodness." When she finished reading she looked up and said with a hint of astonishment, "You have been through quite the journey."

I stared out the window as familiar road signs passed by. I used Google Maps on my phone to verify my locations, as if to dispel any doubt that I was getting farther from my children instead of nearer. I texted Denny with regular updates, as if to dispel any notion in *his* head that my homecoming was a dream. Familiar settings began to appear. When the Southwest Detention Centre showed on the horizon, my heart leaped. Never has anyone been so elated to see a jail. I was finally home. (Windsor, not the jail.)

A small crowd of friends and relatives, my mother among them, was waiting at the Tayfour Regional Rehabilitation Centre parking lot with Welcome Home signs, but due to COVID restrictions I was whisked past them. The testing protocols meant 48 hours would pass until I could have visitors. I had a COVID test before leaving London, but you never know, I thought sarcastically, I *could have caught it on the ambulance ride here.*

From a mental health perspective, it was not the best time to be alone.

The projected release date was Nov. 1 – two weeks away. I was on target to make Halloween.

I continued to suffer separation anxiety from life-support. Where are the monitors that will ring out if I crash? Who is looking after my blood pressure and my heart? What is my white blood cell count? Where are the IVs? In a rehab centre, they generally don't exist.

To calm me, doctors ordered a blood test that showed my white count was normal; I remained infection free. I could start on the therapies that would heal my body, calm my raging anxieties and prepare me to resume a life that was but a faded memory – mom to a newborn, two young boys and a pair of teenage stepkids.

My doctor ordered a halt to the media access that accompanied my return. If it was left to me, I would have talked to everyone. The media had been kind to me throughout my swimming career and medical ordeal. A local magazine, The Drive, posted a welcome home message calling me "without question the strongest woman we've ever met."

"The love, faith, prayers and unbelievable community support have been miraculous. Welcome home Danielle, we've been expecting you."

***

Don't let anyone tell you that an ostomy bag isn't the most dreaded creation in the history of medical science. Not only are its contents disgusting, but it needs regular care. You are constantly on the lookout for leaks. Your clothes don't fit. Luckily for me, Denny became an ostomy expert in London by paying close attention to the artistry of my nurses. He wouldn't heed their advice to leave the room. He watched every step. Every nuance. But Denny had a thousand other things to tend to, including the kids and his impending return to work, so I would need to step up.

I would have to become a Wizard of Os.

I did not relish the task. My state of mind was, literally, shitty. I rejected the assertions of people who said you can live a normal life on a bag. They don't have newborns. *I am different. I am a Paralympic legend and a Pinterest Mom.* Last time I checked, Pinterest Moms don't poop in a bag. There are no Pinterest posts on Ostomy Fashion. My gravestone will not read, "Here lies Danielle. Osto-mom."

I suffered emotional breakdowns – some of my worst since Morgan was born – usually in Denny's arms. The poor guy must have permanent salt stains on his shoulders.

Thank God I survived septic shock but honestly, what the fuck? How am I 36 years old and pooping in a bag? I was in good health and had my baby. And now I'm dealing with the most ridiculous mess.

Three things pulled me back from this abyss:

1. Karen, an angel posing as a nurse, who was about as compassionate an ostomy instructor as they come.

2. Denny, my White Knight, who when I apologized for putting him through bag detail, replied, "Don't apologize. You're here and that's all that matters. I don't care if I have to do this for the rest of our lives as long as I have you."

3. My kids ... and the late October day that I discover them again.

The video conferencing I had relied on to connect with the boys was a Band-Aid. I felt better, sort of, but realized I was drifting further from them. A video mom couldn't meet their needs.

When they arrived at Tayfour for a visit, Corbin, Samson and Morgan were dressed in matching T-shirts inscribed with, "Mom's Our Superhero." Corbin dove into my lap, gently stroking my face and tousling my hair. Sam was more apprehensive. He wasn't even speaking when I had the baby two months ago and to my surprise, had developed a vocabulary.

Corbin asked, "Mommy, can you sing us a song? You used to sing us to bed all the time. I've been waiting to hear you sing."

An emotional wave crashed over me. I hummed a song to my kids.

Corbin said, "Is this real or am I dreaming?"

No, honey, this is real.

"I didn't think you were ever coming back, Mommy. I really thought you were going to Heaven."

We were on the verge of a blubber fest when Corbin flicked a switch, back to kid mode. "Did you bring me any snacks?" Laughter supplanted the tears. I posted to Facebook, *For the first time in a long time things are starting to feel safe again. Having my babies in my arms is the fuel I need to keep pushing through the pain.*

Denny reached new heights as the family's real superhero, visiting rehab morning and afternoon, picking Corbin up from school, having dinner with the kids and bringing Morgan to me for nightly visits. Meanwhile, my maternal connection to my daughter was slow developing because someone else had been caring for her since birth. We had no bond. I nursed her for five days in the hospital, or at least I am told, before it was determined I was too weak.

Now, I didn't know her. I didn't know how she liked to be held. I could not be with her for more than 90 minutes without needing to be relieved so I could collapse in tears. That I ever doubted the need for rehab at Tayfour now struck me as crazy. They nursed my body, but more importantly, breathed life into my soul.

Near the end of rehab, I was strong enough to hold Morgan in my arms. One night, something clicked. She looked up at Denny and, as if to say, "I understand now," gave him a big smile. He said, "Yeah, that's your Mommy." I pulled her in tightly and she nuzzled her head in my side, a deep and warm and wonderful embrace, and it felt like we cemented our bond as mother and daughter.

Her eyes said, "I've been looking for you."

Denny McLeod is with **Danielle Campo McLeod**.
October 20, 2021 · 🌐

Today's post, part 1:
Morgan and mama, back together again.
A little visit while Corbin is in school and Samson is napping.
Outside visit with the boys after school today!
Stay tuned.

Nurses scurried by my window to catch a peak of this union in bloom. You don't often see newborns in a rehab clinic. I was so heartened that I started to press for my release, remembering I promised the boys I would be home for Halloween.

"I'm not putting a date on it," my doctor said, "because I just know that you will beat it. I want you to go home when it feels right to go home."

I asked for a day pass for Oct. 31, but the head nurse said they were not allowed due to COVID protocols. As I was coming to grips with disappointing my kids once again, she flashed a wry grin and announced my discharge. "We all agreed that if you think you are ready, you are ready."

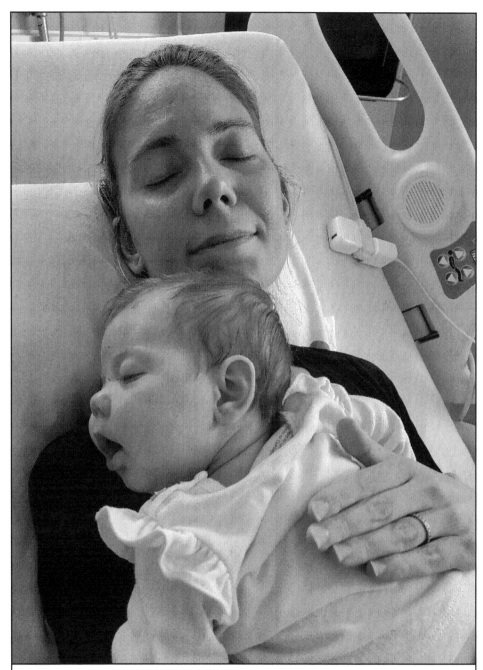

 Denny McLeod
October 20, 2021 · 🌐

•••

Today's post, part 2:
Corbin: "is this really real or a dream?"

Denny picked me up at 7 the morning of the 31ˢᵗ, and by the time the kids emerged from their bedrooms, I was seated on a couch in the living room.

"Really? Really? You're really home Mommy?"

In an instant, we were in trick-or-treat prep mode, as if the last two months had never happened. Denny fashioned a mummy costume for Corbin while Samson's getup would require more creativity. He wanted to be a human excavation machine. Denny worked a minor miracle with a large box – human excavator complete with working lift and scoop.

We scrambled to find candles for the pumpkin because the only ones in the house had been used for prayer vigils. Apprehensive from the last time he pushed me down a sidewalk in a wheelchair, Denny assigned the task to his sister Allison and her husband Brad. They were extra protective as we made our rounds. I asked, What's going on? Why are you being so overbearing? I'm fine. I had no memory of the day I was taken to hospital in septic shock after a painful wheelchair ride to school. Denny posted the most eloquent reflection.

Denny McLeod is with **Danielle Campo McLeod**. •••
October 31, 2021 · 🌐

As we move into November, I reflect on the last couple months of my life. Where I was, where I went, where I am, what could have been and where WE are going. I thank all the powers above us that Danielle is still here to share life with me. It's hard to come to terms with and accept how close I (we all) came to losing her. There would be nothing in this world that wouldn't remind me of her. Whether it be a word, a stretch of road, a song, a smell, a time of year, all this would have been a painful reminder of my love that I lost. A future that wouldn't have been. Our "growing old together" that wouldn't have happened. Everything we planned to do and everything that would have just happened naturally. Things on our 'someday' list that we would have never been able to check off. All so hard to imagine. Thankfully, I can let those thoughts fade into my past and I can focus on our days ahead.

I would like to thank everyone for every bit of support that we have received. It means so much to us.

Onward and upward. I know we still have a long road ahead; I'll be with you every step of the way Danielle. WELCOME HOME!!!

Home life was challenging. After missing 44 days of my children's lives, and with severe physical limits and emotional fragility, I could not simply plug back in. The kids screamed for a glass of water and could not understand why I couldn't get them one. It was Denny who answered the bell when Morgan cried out in the middle of the night.

My house was no longer mine. It was taken over by a never-ending stream of well-intentioned nurses, PSWs and therapists. The kids were off their routines. Denny passed out from exhaustion at the end of the day.

I was a mess, fighting, emotionally, to stay checked in. I used every skillset that I had learned about mental health and wellness. I had moments where I walked to the kitchen window, out of earshot of the children, and lost it. Literally howled with anger and pain. On top of everything that had happened to me, I felt like I was failing my kids. I was providing nothing to them except my presence in the house.

I was in survival mode. The fear that gripped me in London, that I would not live to raise my children, had not gone away. I could not close my eyes without feeling like they wouldn't open again.

Danielle, snap out of it. Fact check. These are your facts. You are not dying.

When you are in survival mode, you can't be a mom. When the kids cried, I was aware that they needed something but physically could not meet their needs. With Samson now talking in sentences, I had to build a relationship despite two months of missing pieces.

Now I had a second child who could express his fear of losing me. "Are you going to have to go back into the hospital Mommy?" My newborn had been raised, and I am eternally grateful to them, by her grandmothers. Now, I had to find a place in her life. But I was not strong enough to breastfeed. Seeing my mother give Morgan a bottle caused resentment and anger.

My baby doesn't even need me.

My strength was slow to return. I had not resumed Mestinon following the breathing issues in London. My blood pressure remained low and I required either a wheelchair or a walker. I could not stand up on my own. I could not shower on my own. My house was full of strangers. And the dreaded ostomy bag continued to haunt my every waking moment. My in-laws Allan and Linda stayed with us for three weeks, and I don't know where I would have been – how deep an abyss I would have sunk into – without them.

My craving for normalcy returned. Our families made incalculable contributions, but a normal couple doesn't rely so much on others. If not for Denny's even temperament, I would have gone insane. But even *he* was growing tired of my constant apologies.

"Stop it. You're here. That's all that matters."

That damn bag. I left the hospital not knowing if the ileostomy could be reversed. In some cases it can't. Karen, my rehab centre nurse and a veteran of wound care who had worked in the U.S., taught me some of the tricks of the trade like eating a marshmallow 20 minutes before changing the bag makes the changeover easier. Who knew? Nurses deserve better nicknames, but Poop Bag Angel would befit Karen.

Denny multi-tasked, simultaneously changing Morgan's poopy diaper and my poopy bag. He was a saint. Me, not so much.

The bag affected everything I ate, everything I wore. The glue ripped at my skin, leaving open sores. For the first time in my life, I used an expression that crossed the line with Denny: *I just can't do it anymore. If this is my forever, just kill me.*

Furious, he replied, "You frickin' find a way to shit in that bag and get over it. This can't be the thing that makes us lose you because you can't emotionally get over it."

I got the message.

In typical McLeod fashion, we found humour in the madness. One day, Samson's potty training thundered to a halt. He stopped asking for the potty. He wanted to follow my example. "Mommy's pooping in a bag. I want to poop in a bag."

The new year brought welcome news from my Windsor surgeon: the ileostomy was reversible and I was strong enough to book a procedure. Though it meant returning to surgery, I didn't hesitate. *Get it off of me!* With the bag starting to cause dehydration and impair my output, and my weight struggling to hold at 90 pounds, removing it could not wait. On March 3, I would return to the operating table.

University Hospital was not an option because COVID had cancelled procedures of this type. Windsor had an opening. I was petrified of going under anesthetic again, but it was worth it to bid adieu to the Pit of Poop.

Two days before the surgery, I had a bedtime conversation with my five-year-old:

"Mommy how many days until you go to the hospital."

Two days

"Oh good, my wishing star is still there. Mommy I'm going to pray every day for you."

Thanks buddy I love you.

"I will miss you Mommy but don't worry. Know what I remember from last time you were in the hospital?"

What Corbin?

"So many people love us and take care of us and Daddy when you are in the hospital."

Corbin, that makes my heart happy.

"Me too Mommy. And Mommy, my wishing star works this time so I'm going to wish you come home faster in less sleeps and you bring chocolate."

Corbin's wish came true. The procedure was performed laparoscopically, without issue, and after a few days I was discharged. My bowels were working properly for the first time since Morgan's birth. *Alleluia!*

Like Mother, Like Son

As I learned in the days after my release, infections are low-down, conniving, cursed creatures, and mine was not through with me yet. Like a B movie rerun, I began to experience pain in my abdomen again. *What the heck is going on?* My internal medicine specialist checked the area around my ribcage and discovered fluids and an abscess. He started antibiotics and I was readmitted to the hospital so the abscess could be drained. I recovered, started to eat solid foods again and after a few days was released.

After a few days at home, the pain was back. A jabbing pain in my ribs. Only this time I refused to acknowledge it. I was sitting in my living room, the kids were playing and I told myself, *You are not going back to the hospital. No way. You're not going back. This is all in your head.*

The look on my face when I admitted to Denny that I was sick again was one of crushing defeat. We returned to the hospital, only to find the abscess filled again. Doctors found E. coli in my bloodstream. Another attempt at draining was followed by an examination by an infectious-disease specialist. He adjusted my meds and almost instantly I felt better. We agreed that I would not leave the hospital until I had been on IV antibiotics for five days. *Great, more time away from the children I'd just been reacquainted with,* I thought. But I was not complaining. We had to put an end to this cycle of infection. And on the bright side, *THE BAG IS GONE!*

Reports of my return to hospital reached the media. By now, I had supporters spanning the globe. They rallied behind me, constantly asking for updates and offering encouragement. "We're sorry you're going through this. You're going to be OK. You're there for a reason. Hang in." When Denny walked the kids to school, strangers pulled over to tell him they were lighting candles again.

My fight against this infection lasted through March. Another month lost in the haze of hospital care. Another month away from my kids.

I was released by the infectious-disease team, removed from antibiotics and was getting ready for Easter when I started feeling sick again. I could not hold down food. Yet again, I was carted from my home in an ambulance. Doctors suspected a kink in the bowel, and the issue was resolved in time for Denny and I to go home that night. We allowed ourselves to think the best.

Maybe this was the end of the story.

Sadly, we were wrong. One week later I was vomiting again and my blood pressure dropped. Mom drove me to the hospital and Denny stayed with the kids. Antibiotics were resumed and a CT ordered. Repeated visits to the X-ray department had made me besties with the imaging staff, and they could not hide the fact that something serious had been detected on my scan. They welled up with tears and couldn't look me in the eye.

I thought, *It's never a good thing when your poker face is a poor attempt to hold back tears. Oh God, they found something.*

My mom reassured me that it was nothing but a hiccup, but the doctor shared a more frightening verdict.

"Danielle, your bowels are OK, but your gall bladder is essentially ready to explode. We will have to admit you."

I had contracted cholestasis, a reduction or stoppage of bile flow. I had my old friend sepsis to thank because the condition was caused by rapid fluctuations in weight. The fluids I absorbed to flush out the sepsis took me from 100 pounds to 200 pounds and back to 84 pounds in two weeks.

I would need surgery to remove the gall bladder but at this point, the organ was too inflamed to do it. I stayed in the hospital long enough to get the infection under control. Then I went home, on antibiotics, and awaited my next dance with the knife. For me, this was a bridge too far. I exploded in an emotional breakdown with my mom. *Please, please make this end. I can't do this fucking roller-coaster anymore. I can't take any more surgery. I just want to be a mom.*

I began to suspect that this was more than a run of bad luck. God was testing me. "What will it take to break you Danielle?" How could I stay positive? What did my kids think, watching me leave them in ambulances? In and out of the hospital like a yo-yo. They were being traumatized. The boys probably blamed their little sister for doing this to their mom. They would need professional help. And where was I? Flat on my back.

You learn a lot about yourself when you nearly die three times. I've been to the angry spot and it doesn't serve a purpose. It just leaves a mark on your soul.

***

By the time I reached University Hospital's emergency ward, on life support, back in September, I had landed on the radar of the Canadian medical research community. Think of it: Muscular dystrophy sufferer becomes elite athlete, has diagnosis revised to myasthenic syndrome, responds to treatment, inexplicably gets pregnant, delivers healthy baby, develops bowel obstruction, contracts sepsis, spends five days in a coma., miraculously survives. Someone should write a book! I am a rare-disease specialist's cornucopia.

Danielle Campo McLeod
April 29 · 🌐

•••

Today is not a good day. I'm back in the hospital and will need surgery. I sit with so many mixed emotions. I'm devastated, I'm scared, and I'm down right lost for words. it's all the little shit you have to deal with when your body is going through medical issues. So I take a deep breath and I focus on the facts.
1. It's not my bowels.
2. It was caught early
3. I'm stronger everyday and healthy
4. I have an incredible support system that steps up and takes care of everything.
5. My husband is my rock and just listening to his breathing grounds me.
6. You reading this post keeps me pushing on.
I will get better my life will be about enjoying all the small things and thanking God for each battle.
But today it's ok to just not be ok. What's the purpose of this test?
But look in my eyes there is still so much fight left.
Time to celebrate the fight...

An estimated three million Canadians with rare diseases navigate lifelong mazes of testing, diagnosis, care and treatment – often alone, according to the Canadian Association for Rare Disorders. It can take five to 10 years to get an accurate diagnosis, and years more to get to the right specialist, with multiple misdiagnoses and sometimes the wrong treatment along the way.

Luckily for me, once I was out of the coma and off life support, a neurological dynamic duo stepped in. I had met Ottawa Hospital's Dr. Jodi Warman Chardon at a conference I attended for Muscular Dystrophy Canada. Supported by Care4Rare, a pan-Canadian collaborative team of clinicians, scientists and researchers focused on improving the care of rare-disease patients, she wanted in on my case for years. I started seeing her before Morgan was born because I wanted a woman's perspective. Once a year we drove to Ottawa for an MRI in what Denny and I called our "poutine trips." My success on Mestinon fascinated her. She wondered if it was an option for other neuromuscular disorders.

Technically I was cheating on Dr. Tarnopolsky, my Hamilton neuro, but by the time I contracted sepsis, questions of professional etiquette were irrelevant. There were larger issues at play, issues that might impact the broader muscular dystrophy community. And my children.

Dr. Michael Nicolle, a neuro at University Hospital, arranged tests to determine if there was more to learn about my condition and its treatment. A week in a coma made me an ideal guinea pig because of the muscle atrophy in my legs. They were literally ripe for testing.

Technicians conducted an EMG, or electromyography, the procedure I endured as a child where needles were injected into my muscles to measure their response to nerve stimulation. It hurt like hell, and coming on the heels of my near death, the suffering was hard to accept. They fired the electrodes seven times, just to be sure.

Ouch. Ouch. Ouch. Ouch. Ouch. Ouch. Ouch.

When she received the results at home in front of her computer, Dr. Warman told her husband to put off dinner for a minute so she could check for abnormalities in my EMG readings. Three hours later, she was in a state of disbelief. The so-called "gigantic" responses that my muscles exhibited told a different tale of my illness.

I didn't have myasthenic syndrome after all. I had spinal muscular atrophy, a completely different gene mutation. It's a neurodegenerative disease that impairs neuromuscular transmission. It was limited to my lower extremities, which explained why vital organs such as my heart and lungs were never harmed. And its discovery would have profound consequences. My children had a 50-50 chance of inheriting it.

My thoughts turned immediately to Samson, my three-year-old. That he stumbled a lot was no longer cute. It was alarming. We had a feeling that something from me was passed down to him.

My childhood was on instant replay. I would relive my mother's ordeal, and worse, it would be my fault. Denny and I lived in worry that it was only a matter of time before we got the diagnosis that confirmed it. And I thought it was easy when it was only me carrying it; I could take a pill. We wondered if we would have made different choices about children had we known. Of course, we would. The kids could have it and be asymptomatic. The uncertainty gnawed at us. We scheduled Corbin, Sam and Morgan to be examined in London.

My tests also ruled out that I inherited my condition from my parents, which was no small relief for them. For years, as a kind of gallows humour/defence mechanism, they had jokingly pointed the finger at each other. "Colleen, your family ate too much butter," Dad would say. Now we knew it was a spontaneous mutation.

Oddly, SMA was one of my original diagnoses as a child, before genetic testing. But my physical development didn't bear it out. So, doctors landed on fibro disproportion and off we went. I had a classic form of muscular dystrophy, they thought.

New diagnosis 2.0 led to some mind-boggling questions, not the least of which: If I didn't have myasthenic syndrome, and my body responded to Mestinon, is it an option for my new diagnosis? While clinical trials have explored whether the drug is effective for spinal muscular atrophy, results have never been definitive enough for it to be prescribed. The small silver lining was that my case would be added to that body of research that may give others a better life. At least I could hang my hat on that.

The other unanswered question was, why have my pain and weakness not returned to their former levels in the nearly one year since I stopped taking Mestinon? I was not as strong as I was on the drug, but the difference was insubstantial. I had to focus more when carrying out physical tasks, as if supervising the conversation between my nerves and muscles. In order to use a pen, I needed to order my fingers to move. But I was not nearly as debilitated as before.

Dr. Warman could not explain it, and when she suggested that five days in a coma may have served as a "reset button," she was not entirely kidding.

It took me much longer than an able-bodied person to restore my muscle function following the coma – literally days for each finger and toe. Coughing. Speaking. A battle of mind over matter to sit up straight. It wasn't like flipping the switches of an electrical panel. I required a spectrum of assistive devices. My mother produced videos of me before Morgan's birth to give doctors a baseline understanding of what they were trying to wake up.

As I awaited gall bladder surgery, memories of that difficult recovery left me terrified.

OK, now I have SMA and it is progressive. What does that mean when they put me under?

I worried, *Will my daughter walk the path my mother did, losing her mom before we walk her down the aisle?*

The kids were booked for an assessment by a pediatric neuromuscular specialist at Victoria Hospital in London, where many of my childhood examinations took place. Thinking it was introductory, we agreed to have Denny stay home and work and have my mother accompany me. Not until we arrived did we learn that the hospital was planning to conduct the dreadful, painful, nightmare-inducing EMG on my children, the same test that had driven me to tears as a child and after I recovered from sepsis.

Passing through the same hospital entrance as in my childhood reopened an old wound for Mom and when she saw me clutching three EMG authorization sheets, she cried out, "Not happening!"

She was right. I couldn't subject them to the pain. Surely, there had to be a better way. They didn't need to be zapped and it certainly wouldn't happen without Denny there. Was this all about gathering data? My kids won't be lab rats. I have SMA. I'm pretty sure Samson does too. A physical exam would confirm what we already knew.

They're not having an EMG today. Period.

When the specialist agreed to shelve the EMG for a physical examination, Corbin and Morgan displayed normal neuromuscular function. But when the exam turned to Samson, my sweet, gentle, innocent boy, things I had never noticed – or had turned a blind eye to – became obvious. He fell far more often than I recalled. He couldn't stand up like my other two, needing his arms for support.

The doctor looked at me and said, in an echo of 35 years ago, "He has a form of muscular dystrophy. For sure he does." But when she observed that he had "the best possible mom" to guide him because of my life experiences, it struck me as hollow. My life might have been great, but the highs did not come without suffering. I did not want that for Sam.

SMA manifests itself in quick, sudden declines. He could leap into bed one night and wake up needing a wheelchair. We won't know for years how it will play out. In the meantime, we will follow the same course as my parents did with me – focus on building the muscles that are strong. Get him into the pool.

Significantly, Dr. Warman predicted that, given the pace of scientific research and the multitude of clinical drug trials, a treatment would come in Samson's lifetime.

Still, the diagnosis was like a blindfold had been removed from my eyes – all the times I had seen Sam struggle and unconsciously served as protector by making the playground toys easier to access, removing him from the pool before he got tired, asking his older brother to slow down in a game of tag. Now I understood why he napped for three hours every afternoon – his muscles needed recovery time. Now, when he tells me his legs hurt, I retreat to a hidden corner and cry.

When we left the hospital, the kids were exhausted. Two had pooped their pants and I was emotionally drained. We pulled into the McDonald's drive-through and ordered Happy Meals while I dialled Denny to share news that both of us had expected.

To my surprise, Denny was relieved. "Oh, thank God," he said. "I've been sitting here terrified thinking they would say it is something worse. We can deal with what we know. We knew he had it; we just didn't say it out loud." How fortunate we are, he said, that when we started thinking about having kids, we didn't know I had a form of MD that had a 50 per cent chance of being passed down. Corbin, Sam and Morgan would not be in our lives today. Sam is strong – stronger than I was at that age – and we have a blueprint for giving him a normal life.

"Would you change anything?" Denny asked.

Thinking my husband hadn't grasped the significance of the diagnosis, I was frustrated. I didn't want to be reminded of the obstacles I had overcome. I was fixated on the obstacles Sam would face. I don't want the other kids to play Ditch Sam.

"I can't be angry at this. I just can't," Denny said. "Look at how you have learned to survive things. Look at this person you have become. We will deal with this. The world is a different place." He was right: Modern society would not condone a cruel invention like Ditch Danielle or slurs like gimp and cripple. We had the world's heightened sensitivities working for us. At least that was something.

Later, standing in the cool Lake Huron waters at Bayfield, where we stopped after Sam's diagnosis to see my folks at their cottage, I said to Sam, *Mommy will always take care of you. I have already been where you are going. I have walked these steps. All you have to do is walk in my footsteps.*

To which my three-year-old replied, "I'll just walk on your toes." And by the way, "You have sand in your mouth."

Feeling a strong urge to reunite with Denny, I scrapped plans to stay overnight and bundled the kids into the minivan for the two-hour drive home. Mom offered to join me but I declined. I needed a captain-of-the ship moment. Bad call.

Halfway home, the large coffee that launched my day was starting to give me an urge. Should I pull over at the final rest stop, with three young children in tow, or power through? If I am meant to stop, please God, send me a sign.

On cue, Morgan filled her diaper, prompting Corbin to cry out, "It smells so bad!" Sam chimed in: "I pooped long times ago. It's on my legs."

Pulling off the highway, and never having done a solo pit stop with the three kids, I second-guessed my decision. The thought crossed my mind that I could park the minivan off to the side of the lot, leave the kids strapped inside and pee by a tree. Except, there were no trees. No bushes. Not even a patch of overgrown grass. It was either go inside or borrow a diaper from Morgan.

The family washroom was disgusting but I had reached the point of no return. Down went my yoga pants as I sternly warned the kids not to touch anything.

Another bad call.

Family washrooms in rest stops are wheelchair accessible. Wheelchair accessible doors are opened mechanically with large buttons that might attract the attention of a mischievous three-year-old. Once the opening starts, it can't be stopped. Sam flashed his mischievous "I'm-gonna-touch-something" smile and I cringed:

Oh my God!

Oh my God!!

Oh my God!!!

Before you could say, "Free Show," Sam whipped around and smacked the automatic door opener. I shrieked. The toilet seat I was occupying directly faced the door that was now passing, like my life, before me. In a flash, I was flashing. Three men passed by and couldn't help but check out the half-naked blond with the one-year-old in her arms, and I was powerless to stop the exhibition. I waddled to the door but it could not be forced shut.

"Oh, you poor thing," a woman cried out, to which I replied, *Yeah, right. Have kids, they said.*

The first thought that crossed my mind was, if I was going to put myself on display, I might as well have peed by a tree. The second was, how appropriate that the perpetrator of my most embarrassing life moment was the little boy who had begun to consume so much of my sympathy. No. Forget that. He will be fine. He will make shit happen.

It struck Denny that my washroom tour-de-force was the perfect ending to an awful day. It was typical of how our family copes with difficulties like Sam's diagnosis. A traumatizing event is followed by a ridiculous debacle that takes away the sting. "All this stuff you went through," he said, "and it's the bathroom door you'll remember most."

Morgan's Messy Miracles

Dinner at the McLeod house is a symphony of chaos; Morgan firing baby-food projectiles from her highchair, Corbin and Samson spinning laps around the table, Ella and Calum doing teenager cool. We call our meals "a gathering of the herd" because the kids act like wild animals. Before a single morsel is consumed, like clockwork, one of the younger ones spills something. A glass of milk. A bowl of soup. The pickle jar. *Cleanup on Aisle 5!*

Denny locks eyes with me and deadpans, "You are so damn lucky you didn't leave me with this!" That he says it in front of the kids is no big deal, and in fact elicits agreement from 17-year-old Calum. "Yeah, Dad, that would have been a nightmare."

Never a day passes where Denny doesn't make me feel that our relationship is the most important thing in his life. He says he could not have raised the kids without me, but in fact, he would have done it masterfully. I marvel at his resilience. Because of my many disappearances, and because they are old enough to grasp that I am unwell, the kids regard Denny as their constant. I'm still working to build a relationship with Morgan; to replace the blocks I couldn't put in place after her birth and the diversion of my energy since then to survival. While Morgan's resilience is welcome as a mom, I often wish she were more dependent on me. I feel disposable to her. I catch myself watching her interaction with Denny, holding his face in her hands and staring into his eyes as if to say, "I know what's coming, Dad. We've got this."

What I know of my daughter's first days is a construct. Bits and pieces, photos and Facebook posts, random observations from Denny and my mom that I have cobbled together but do not yet seem genuine. They feel more like a checklist of things you do for your child simply to say you did. It can feel empty. The sadness of those missing three months creeps in from time to time, but I do not allow it to stay long. My family understands my need to fill the mortar in our foundation and as a result will defer to me when I insist on giving Morgan her bottle. Daycare? I couldn't put her there.

While I was still in the hospital my mother instilled in me the need to build the bond. A friend of hers, who is a child psychologist, advised us to leave an item in my hospital bed that would be passed on to Morgan. Today she searches her crib for her Winnie the Pooh blanket.

"Yes, it's important to build her attachment to you," the psychologist said. "But it's equally important that you see she needs it, because the blanket represents you."

Corbin and Sam are also works in progress. Sam will need a modern support system to walk my path of disability; Corbin needs his faith renewed that I am not leaving him. When he started behaving aggressively toward Sam, a child psychologist diagnosed him with adjustment disorder, which is an emotional or behavioural reaction to a stressful event – like your mom's life-threatening illness. His version of it, as related to the psychologist, is that when I delivered Morgan, she took my insides out and forgot to put them back. If I am not in his presence, he can't accept that I'm OK. He calls out from his bedroom, "Mommy, you still alive?" *Yes Corbin, Mommy is still alive. You can go to sleep now.*

With Denny at my side, I can do this. No wonder the sound of his voice awakened me. He makes me feel grounded and safe. When he refused to say goodbye, it wasn't showing off for my family. He was making a pledge for life.

I feel that while I often tell him I love you, I don't often enough say *I appreciate you.*

The boys usher in their day by saying good morning to their sister, whom they call Morgie, fighting over a chair at the breakfast table and firing up their iPads. Morgan plays in her crib, always smiling and often emerging with a face full of paint chips she gnawed from its railings.

On Aug. 17, 2022, we celebrated Morgan's first birthday. While some might be inclined to dwell on a difficult year, we parked those reflections for a day. We invited 40 people to the house, many of them Corbin's friends and their parents, and proceeded to demolish our yard. We hung piñatas full of Hubba Bubba bubble gum and suckers, rubber duckies with unicorn horns for Morgan and toy frogs for Corbin. We used COVID facemasks as blindfolds to avoid sharing. Corbin complained that he couldn't see (duh, that's the point) and

Samson was stung in the ear by a bee.

We ordered three king pizzas (32-piece) and ended up needing five. The two bonus pizzas arrived quickly because the restaurant we deal with had followed our case in the media and, as the delivery person said, "the whole place was praying for you." When we called to order donuts, a girl at the bakery cried to learn she was part of Morgan's 1st. One hundred and sixty pizza slices, four dozen donuts, two cases of pop, two dozen juice boxes and 50 bags of potato chips and assorted fruit cups and veggie trays were no match for this herd.

The boys wore T-shirts saying, "Bros of the Birthday Princess." We started a tradition of buying Denny a bottle of Scotch so he can toast his daughter. I selected Glenfiddich Project XX Experimental Series – the black label, box and bottle seemed appropriate. The boys bought their sister flowers and a card. When they fought over each giving her individual cards, I cut it in two.

Our umbrella stand broke and Denny drilled holes in a wooden table to secure it. At a lunch with the grandparents, the boys sang Happy Birthday and Morgan decorated her face with cheesecake. When the other children arrived it was chaos. The trampoline was destroyed – Denny thought it deliberate on my part to score a new one – and our lawn was mangled by the toy cars that used it as a speedway.

While the parents gossiped and the children slammed piñatas, Morgan, who is graced with a daredevil spirit, spent much of the party being propelled down the driveway in a plastic car. She sat in her walker eating a peanut butter and jelly sandwich then used her snaggle tooth to gnaw on a pizza crust. When it was time for bed, her hair was plastered to her head by a sticky substance we never identified.

For many of the children, it was their first full-blown birthday party since Christmas. "It's like a recess that never ends," one said gleefully. While it was billed as an open house, everyone arrived at the designated start time – 4:30 – and no one left until it ended at 9:30. By then, Morgan and Sam were sleeping and Corbin was a zombie.

No speeches. No solemn moments. Only Sam, tasked with thanking everyone for coming, actually thanking them for *going*.

It was a loud, rowdy and as messy as a Campo bun fight. It was perfect. Afterward, Denny and I browsed through photographs from 365 days ago, before my illness, and decided to focus on the happiness before the storm. One of the photos was a nurse holding newborn Morgan in front of a clock that read 7:45 a.m. Another was me nursing her, which I did albeit briefly. We focused on the day she was born – a great day. Everything else can be saved for another time.

To those who gave me cards and flowers, or who looked me in the eye and asked with a crook in their expression, "How are you doing?" I thought, save that for Sept. 11. And give some of that compassion to Denny.

I said to him, *We're one step closer to dancing at her wedding.* It was my way of fact-checking: *What do I know right now? Right now, it's her first birthday. Nothing else matters. I can put the blinders around everything else.*

Because my illness played out so publicly, not a week passes without an email or text from someone thanking me for inspiring them. I understand it. But being an inspiration is also a responsibility. Do I believe my survival was a miracle? Yes, absolutely. And that is a gift I am happy to share. I am not a saviour, but if my message has healing powers, I offer it wholeheartedly.

We left our year of living dangerously with the goal of giving back to the community that supported us through my ordeal. When the finances allow, we will establish a foundation for families who go through unexpected turmoil. We will call it "Morgan's Messy Miracles" and the slogan will read, "Because shit happens." It seems appropriate. We didn't plan any of the misfortune that hit us – it just got messy.

"Only you," said Denny, "would turn something about poop into a way to give back."

While some may consider me cursed by a burden, I consider myself blessed with a mission. Not everyone gets one. My will to survive, which was forged in the cauldron of Paralympic training, burns stronger than ever. I have been told many times that I would not make it, only to prove the doubters wrong. Know this: I AM NOT FINISHED. Not by a longshot. I will establish Danielle Campo Inc., a wellness consultancy. I will witness Morgan's first steps. I will teach my kids to swim. I will well up with pride when they take their sacraments. I will cheerlead when they graduate college. I will shed tears when Denny walks Morgan down the aisle, then party like a rock star at the reception.

I will celebrate the community that rallied around me and dedicate my life to helping others find their pathways to wellness, just as the prayers and candles from perfect strangers illuminated mine.

Epilogue

On Aug. 25, 2022, Danielle underwent successful surgery to remove her gall bladder and rebuild her abdominal wall, which were damaged when she was treated for sepsis. At the date of this memoir's publication she was recovered, back home with Denny and the kids, thankful that shit didn't happen.

It's OK To...

... have passion. But that's the first step. You must live passion to have action.

... let others shoulder your burden. Your strength isn't gone. It's just temporarily inaccessible.

... take a minute to pause, breathe and fact check before making a panicked decision.

... fail and fail again, and not be afraid to admit it. Life is a journey of discovery, not a final exam.

... cut yourself some slack. Obsessing with perfection is exhausting, because you run and run, but never arrive.

... feel a community's love and pay it back. You are loved and supported more than you know.

... believe in a higher power. We're not alone, and miracles do happen. You are so worth it.

... turn a dead end into a way forward. In the face of obstacles, you will find the candles that illuminate your path.

Love, Danielle

Thursdays With Marty

My collaborator, Marty Beneteau, is founder of the Windsor Writers Group and former Publisher and Editor in Chief of The Windsor Star. In his 35-year newspaper career, Marty's teams produced nationally recognized investigations into child welfare, mental health and the healthcare system. Over a span of nearly eight months, we sat on his deck and talked, over coffee and the occasional peanut butter and jelly sandwich. The memories poured out of me as the hours flew by, and Marty magically wove them into my life story. We now consider ourselves friends. I cherish the memories, laughs and tears of Thursdays with Marty.

Gratitude

Mom and Dad, thank you for never leaving my side. It seems cliche to say I don't have the words, but I truly can't express my love and gratitude.

When I married Denny, not only did I receive his two unbelievable children, but two parents who love me like their own. Allan and Linda became my in-laws by default but my friends by choice. I couldn't complete this story without taking a moment to give special acknowledgement to Mom and Dad McLeod.

Our children spent every night in the comfort of their own beds while I fought for my life in hospital. Their every need was met with love and grace. Their wellbeing didn't skip a beat. Linda and Allan became an extension of Denny and me.

At times they felt torn not being at my side, and by their son's side in some of his most difficult and scary moments. They knew that caring for our children was exactly what we needed, and they did it in the most special way. The comfort it gave Denny and me was a gift of incalculable value.

As we move on and heal from this experience, Denny and I see the effects of the trauma on each of our kids. Without question, it would have been worse had Linda and Allan not been there for them.

I must have won the lottery to have in my corner my parents Colleen and Steve, brothers Craig and Kenny, sister-in-law Tricia, nephew Leelan and niece Aria Campo; Allan, Linda, Denny's sister Allison Smith and her husband Brad; our many aunts, uncles and cousins. Denny and I are blessed with incredible friends all over the world.

Thank you to the many doctors, nurses and therapists who guided my path and brought me healing. To everyone who lit a candle, said a prayer, an intention or special act of kindness, thank you for bringing me home to my family.

–Danielle Campo McLeod

Gratitude

Early in the process of writing this memoir, a publisher, Dan Wells, asked how I would know when the story was finished. Danielle was recovering from her latest health scare and preparing for her next surgery. She was awaiting a new diagnosis which might impact her children. There were days when she looked exhausted; days when I worried because I couldn't reach her.

On the morning after our first interview, she texted me that she had gone directly from Starbucks to the hospital with an inflamed gall bladder. She needed it removed and joked that if she died on the operating table, which she feared, we would sell more books. It saddened me, but I understood that humour was her defence mechanism. On the morning of her surgery, she sent me recorded goodbyes to share with her children and parents in the event she didn't make it.

I told Dan Wells, we'll know the story is over when Danielle is sure her kids will have a mom. Now, that chapter of Danielle's life is closed and the story is ready to be told. I offer my deepest thanks to Danielle for entrusting it to me. It has rekindled my love of writing and enriched my life.

Many helped us along the way, most inspirationally Denny, the glue who continues to put Danielle's broken pieces back together, and my wife Nancy, who offered sage wisdom on the touchiest of subjects, made PBJs to tide us over in our marathon sessions and only in extreme cases, insisted I close my laptop and go to bed. Danielle and I are each blessed with life partners who offer us unconditional love and the occasional boot in the ass.

Danielle is inspired by her children Calum, Ella, Corbin, Samson and Morgan, the foundations of her strength and faith. I am similarly blessed by my son Michael and daughter-in-law Gina. Thank you Mike and G.

We couldn't have completed Resurrections without our copy editor Jim Potter and graphic designer Dave Houle, who brought passion, patience and skill to the project, photographer Syx Langemann for the incredible cover photo and guest reader Janice Forsyth, a motivator extraordinaire.

Words can't describe our appreciation for the Windsor-Essex County community that rallied around Danielle. For those who walk in her footsteps – be it chronic pain, bullying, difficulty fitting in, misdiagnosis, a life-threatening illness or dealing with an unexpected struggle – we hope you find inspiration in her story.

This memoir is dedicated to the Jerry's Kid in all of us.

– Marty Beneteau

Danielle's Awards and Achievements

Paralympics (2000, 2004): 3 gold, 2 silver, 2 bronze, 3 world records

Paralympic World Championships (1998, 2002):
7 gold, 3 silver, 1 bronze, 4 world records

Commonwealth Games (2002): 1 bronze

Swim Ontario Aquatic Hall of Fame (2013)

Windsor Essex Sports Hall of Fame (2010)

Terry Fox Humanitarian Award (2005)

King Clancy Award (2005)

Queen Elizabeth II Golden Jubilee Medal (2002)

Queen Elizabeth II Diamond Jubilee Meda (2012)

Dr. W. Kenneth Jaggs Community Award (2002)

Order of Ontario (2001)

Appendix

Follow Danielle on Facebook **@DanielleCampo4**

and Instagram **@d.campo.mcleod**

Visit her website at **daniellecampo.com**

Learn more about muscular dystrophy at **muscle.ca**

Learn more about congenital myasthenic syndromes at
rarediseases.org/rare-diseases/congenital-myasthenic-syndromes

Learn more about spinal muscular atrophy at
my.clevelandclinic.org/health/diseases/14505-spinal-muscular-atrophy

Learn more about sepsis and septic shock at
mayoclinic.org/diseases-conditions/sepsis/symptoms-causes

Learn more about postpartum depression at
camh.ca/en/health-info/mental-illness-and-addiction-index/postpartum-depression

Learn more about the Canadian Organization for Rare Disorders (CORD) at
raredisorders.ca

Learn more about firefighters raising money for MD at
muscle.ca/take-action/fire-fighters

Check out Alison Dilworth's art at **alisondilworth.com**

Watch a video of the capture, tagging and release of
Mary Lee, the great white shark, at
youtube.com/watch?v=Z9_GJlohhoI

Follow Mary Lee on Twitter **@MaryLeeShark**